Searching
for
Normalcy

by

Steven G. Chance

Searching
for
Normalcy

**A young man with cerebral palsy
discovers the sufficiency of God's grace.**

by **Steven G. Chance**

**Preface by Jay Kesler
Forward by Ted Engstrom**

Cross Reference Books
Mt. Juliet, Tennessee

Searching for Normalcy
Copyright © 1996 by Steven G. Chance

The accounts in this book are real, although some names and
circumstances have been altered to protect the privacy of certain
individuals.

Cover design by Charles Carpenter
Back cover photo by Scott Waln

Library of Congress Cataloging-in-Publication Data
Chance, Steven G. 1958-
    Searching for Normalcy/Steven G. Chance.

ISBN 0-89989-232-9
1. Cerebral Palsy   2. Christian Ministry   3. Handicapped

Published by Cross Reference Books
Mt. Juliet, Tennessee
Printed in the United States of America

To Randi,
my wife and best friend.

Table of Contents

Acknowledgments

When I first began work on this book, I was overwhelmed by the seemingly insurmountable task of creating an entire volume of work from start to finish. I lacked the skills of an experienced author and, although I knew I had much to say, found it difficult to put my thoughts on paper. This book could not have been written, therefore, without the support and assistance of many friends and colleagues.

My mother-in-law, Sue Smith, a professional manuscript editor, edited the early drafts of the text and taught me a great deal about some of the more technical aspects of writing.

The Reverend Robert Hill, professional writer and editor, provided me with invaluable suggestions regarding chapter organization and writing style, as well as edited various drafts of this book.

Three friends and fellow Taylor University alumni, Jeff Evans, Jack Hill, and Dan Pederson, have been instrumental in bringing the book to market.

Dottie Coleman has faithfully served me for years as my secretary and friend and has provided countless hours of clerical assistance.

I wish to thank my parents, Elmer and Wanda Chance, along with my brother, Bill Chance, for always believing in me and encouraging me to take risks, even though those risks at times took me far from home.

I wish to also thank the members of the board of directors of Golden Clay Ministries for their faithful service, guidance, and encouragement. Whereas every person who has ever served as a member of the board has made valuable and significant contributions to this ministry, I wish to make special mention of Roland Elder, whose premature death from liver cancer prevented him from seeing this book in print.

I owe a great debt of gratitude to Golden Clay Ministries' many financial supporters. Their generosity has provided me with a platform to develop many of the ideas found in this book.

Finally, I want to thank my wife, Randi, who has stood beside me from the beginning of this project. She is my best friend and has been intricately involved in developing, editing, and proofreading the manuscript.

Steven G. Chance

Preface

When I think of Steve Chance I'm reminded of the words of the apostle Paul, "For when I am weak, then I am strong" (II Cor. 12:10, RSV). From a human vantage point, Steve is among the "weak" ones. He has lived with cerebral palsy and has done so, like many others, with courage and determination. His story is different in that, during his years of struggle, he has refused weak and shallow answers including, the worst kind of all, the religious ones. Steve refuses to rob God of his attributes in order to accommodate his particular case. Steve sees his disability as a part of the human condition and readily acknowledges that the suffering of humanity cannot be conveniently ignored nor silenced by making certain questions taboo. He has asked all of the questions, yet with a stubbornness reminiscent of ancient Job, has refused to admit to things that are simply not true.

Books about suffering are not particularly popular, especially among those who by circumstances find themselves relatively free from pain, hardship, injustice, tragedy, or calamity; however, sooner or later "into each life some rain must fall." When this happens, and when through our abilities, ingenuity, or influence we cannot fix our problems, then we must face up to the questions addressed in this book. Steve cannot escape his body nor stop the involuntary jerks and spasms that frighten others and distance them from easy relationships with him. They are the facts of his life, and these facts set the tone for this useful and theologically mature book. For me, the book has special significance, because I have watched Steve with great interest since my son Bruce's college days at Taylor University, when he began to speak of his greatly gifted friend, Steve Chance. Bruce's initial impressions and our family's respect for Steve have lasted through the years. This book is a document of a man created in the image of God, stripped of the superficialities that often keep us from seeing the real essence of the divine imprint.

> Jay Kesler
> President
> Taylor University

Foreword

All over the world, people are marginalized by debilitating limitations that make normalcy, in the traditional sense of the term, unattainable. They wonder how a loving God can allow people to experience such agonizing hurt, pain that just will not go away. *Searching for Normalcy* was written for those who ask God for change—and are still waiting.

Steve Chance has earned the right to speak to the issue of unanswered questions. As you read through the following pages, you will encounter a man who grew up different from those around him. His playmates noticed. His teachers noticed. The girls noticed. Steve's cerebral palsy has forced him throughout his life to wrestle with the question—what does it mean to be normal?

Steve asks other questions as well—questions that all of us ask. Where is God when tragedy strikes? When I feel worthless? When others reject me? His answers will surprise you and encourage you.

His story will touch your life. Steve is well known as an overcomer. His achievements are many. He has excelled in the classroom. He is a compelling speaker. And now, in his first book, he has proven himself to be a gifted writer.

If you have a disability, you need this book. If you know someone with a disability, you need this book. If you, like me, do not have a disability, yet wrestle with your own "thorn in the flesh," then you too need this book.

And when you finish reading it, share this book with a friend. You'll get a hearty thank you in return!

> Ted Engstrom
> President Emeritus
> World Vision

Introduction

My mother, Wanda Hughes Chance, was 20 years old and in perfect health on the morning I was born, August 12, 1958. She had entered the Beloit Memorial Hospital, in Beloit, Wisconsin shortly after midnight. Six and a half hours later, during the delivery process, trouble began. I was halfway down the birth canal when the doctor realized that I was in a breech position and that my head was too large. My air supply was cut off. I was turning blue and would have died except for the doctor's quick work. As it was, five minutes elapsed between the time I started choking and the time I took my first breath. I was alive but started breathing too late to prevent the brain damage that left me disabled.

It became obvious as early as six months later that something was wrong with me. I lacked any coordination and lagged behind other babies my age in developmental milestones. The doctors blamed my slow development on laziness. They insisted that I was only going through a stage and would undoubtedly grow out of it, given enough time. Each visit to the hospital left my parents more confused and yet more determined to continue their search for some plausible explanation of my difficulties. Finally, after two years of listening to unfounded medical opinions, they heard the answer from a specialist trained in childhood orthopedic dis-

diagnosis was cerebral palsy—undoubtedly, he
of oxygen starvation at birth.

I've never experienced life as a "normal" person, if such a person exists, so I do not know what it's like to live without a disability. Most folks see the visible effects of my cerebral palsy—the gait of my walk, the jerkiness of my arms and hands, and the slowness of my speech. People who spend time with me also know that cerebral palsy affects my everyday activities, from the way I eat breakfast and dress myself in the morning to the way I brush my teeth before going to bed at night.

As difficult as the obvious hurdles of having a disability are, they don't begin to compare with the hidden effects of cerebral palsy. Cerebral palsy affects the way I see myself as a person, the way I relate to other people, and even the way I view God. Nothing I ever do, no one I ever meet, or nothing I ever think is unaffected by the fact that I am disabled.

If, by reading this book, you're expecting to find the story of a disabled man who conquers all of his difficulties with an unshakable faith in Jesus Christ, you will be disappointed. I do profess Christ as my savior. Nevertheless, I am also the type of guy who asks a lot of questions. Believing in God doesn't automatically make life easier and often makes the questions harder to answer. Why, for example, did God allow me to be born with cerebral palsy? This question might be easy for some people to answer, but for me it goes directly to the root of who God is.

Where was this loving God on the first day of my life, when I needed him most? Did he go out to the back nine for an early-morning round of golf, only to return to the clubhouse too late to check his messages? Maybe he had stayed up late the night before, watching *The Tonight Show*. Perhaps he hit the snooze button on the alarm clock once too often and, by the time he showered and dressed, had time to do only half a job. He saved me from dying but was too late to do anything about the cerebral palsy.

I'm ashamed to even think that God didn't care about what happened to me on the morning of my birth. That in all the things God had to take care of, I somehow got lost in the shuffle, and he never took the time to either prevent or fix this disability called cerebral palsy.

Don't get me wrong. I am extremely grateful for the life that I have. But being grateful doesn't take away the shame that comes from being different. It also doesn't take away the one question that has haunted me for years: Where was God during those five crucial minutes I spent trying to take my first breath of air?

I know many people would prefer that I live on blind faith instead of exploring my doubts about God. They believe that questioning whether God is responsible for the pain and suffering of the world borders on heresy and has no place in the Christian faith. They're convinced that nothing good can come from raising such pointed questions and would prefer that I keep mine to myself.

I understand their concern. I, too, am uncomfortable asking these questions, simply because I am afraid of where the answers might lead me. Will they bring me closer to God, or will they push me away from him? I don't know. What I do know is that once I've asked the questions, I cannot simply blot them out of my memory and pretend they never existed. To do so would be dishonest, because no matter how hard I try to ignore the questions, they never go away.

Blind faith doesn't work for me. It never has. I reject the notion that it's wrong to question one's beliefs. There must be room in the Christian faith for people to ask penetrating questions, especially if those questions are directed toward God. I do want answers, because the answers to my questions have a direct bearing on the way I relate to him now that I am an adult. Wherever God was during the time of my birth, he now expects me to have a personal relationship with him. That's just a little hard to swallow if I suspect that he is ultimately responsible for my having cerebral palsy. Why should I worship the God who apparently deserted me on the delivery table?

Although I hope I can find answers, I probably will never resolve these questions completely. That's okay. The important thing is that I face my questions and doubts—to be honest with myself and with God. I've spent a good part of my life searching for normalcy, trying to pretend to myself and the rest of the world that I'm not really disabled—that I'm not different from most other people. It is essential to my mental and spiritual health that I learn to see myself as I am. I must face my imperfections and weaknesses, and I must learn what it means to bring the shame of having cerebral palsy to God.

Included in this book are many stories about my life, from my childhood and school days, to my dating experiences, to my professional life, and more. I have attempted to become as vulnerable as possible on these pages, in hope that my readers will finish the book feeling almost as if they have met and conversed with me in person. My imperfections may be more noticeable than most other people's, yet everyone feels shame—that sense of never being good enough and always falling short of expectations. It's a part of being human. If, by reading these pages, my readers gain an understanding of what it means to be a person with a disability, and then come to better understand the pain, weakness, and grace in their own lives, I will have succeeded in my goal as an author.

One

Walking Like the Tin Man

I was two years old when Mom and Dad learned that I had cerebral palsy. We lived in a small, two-bedroom mobile home in South Beloit, Illinois just a couple of miles south of the Wisconsin state line.

After the diagnosis of cerebral palsy was made, I went overnight from being a kid who was just a little slow to a kid whose whole life was regimented around every type of therapy imaginable. Day after day, week after week, month after month, and year after year, I did whatever it took to try to be just as normal as the next kid. Speech therapy, physical therapy, occupational therapy—I did it all.

Nothing ever came easy to me, no matter how simple the job looked. Most people cannot imagine the time that I needed to do the simplest tasks. Just to put on a pair of socks took ten minutes! Each movement had to be carefully planned ahead of time. Before I could even think about pulling a sock up around my ankle, it first had to go over my toes, down my foot, and around my heel—a relatively simple task for most folks but nearly insurmountable for me. I had to figure out not only where each of my fingers went in order to pull the sock on but also where best to sit to keep from falling over. It sometimes seemed as though all I had to do was breathe, and I would lose my balance. Getting dressed took at least half an hour, and that was after Mom had set me on the couch, handed me my clothes, and pulled my pants up around my knees.

I wore leg braces underneath my pants, and they were the ugliest things you ever saw. Each brace was permanently attached to a shoe and extended all the way up the length of my leg. They came with two leather straps; one buckled at the top of my legs, and the other fastened just below my knees. They were designed with locks that, when engaged, prevented my legs from bending. I hated those braces, especially when they were locked. They were heavy and uncomfortable and made a clanging sound whenever my knees knocked together. I looked a little like a poster child for the March of Dimes and walked like the Tin Man in *The Wizard of Oz*.

Now, you might think that with all the problems I had getting dressed, the least Mom could do would be to tie my shoelaces for me. She tied them all right, but only after I had tied square knots several times while trying to make a bow. Sometimes my brother, Bill, tied the knot for me. But can you imagine the frustration of having your younger brother do in ten seconds what you can't do in five minutes? I was thankful for his help, but I was also embarrassed to be forced to accept that kind of assistance from a brother two years younger than myself. It seems to me that I should have been the one helping him with things instead of the other way around. I was so glad when they started putting Velcro on tennis shoes. If only they had done so thirty years ago! It would have saved me a lot of trouble, not to mention time and frustration.

Have you ever tried eating Jell-O with chopsticks while rollerskating down a gravel road? That's kind of what it's like for me to eat an entire meal without making a mess. I love to eat. Getting the food from the plate to my mouth, that's the tricky part. They say that practice makes perfect, and although I've not totally perfected my eating skills, I have improved with age. But when I was a kid, meals were a major production, and making a mess at the kitchen table was just something I took for granted.

Everyone made eating look so simple. All I had to do was put the food on my spoon, bring the spoon to my mouth, pull out the spoon, chew, and swallow. Nothing to it, right? Wrong! I could get the food onto my spoon, but once I lifted the spoon off the plate, the food was gone. We're talking food everywhere—the table, the floor, my lap, my brother's lap, even the walls. By the end of the meal I was lucky if half the food I started out with made it to my mouth. I was very thin as a kid, and I'm sure that one of the reasons I was so skinny is that I had to work so hard at eating. I earned my food, every bite of it.

The one food I hated most in the whole world was Jell-O. That is without a doubt the all-time hardest stuff to eat. There should be a law permanently banning it from anyplace frequented by people with cerebral palsy. The television advertisement even encouraged kids to "see it wiggle." Just what I needed, a food that wiggles. All I had to do was look at Jell-O and it started moving. Did you notice that I referred to Jell-O in the past tense? That's not by accident. Once I became an adult, no one could tell me what to eat. And since Jell-O was never one of my favorite foods anyway, I stopped eating it. It just isn't worth the effort.

Jell-O may be at the top of my list of the most difficult foods to eat, but peas are a close second. Those babies have a mind of their own. One small shove and they are off the plate, across the table, and onto the lap of the person sitting next to me. I hate it when that happens, especially when I'm at a restaurant with someone I've just met. It's embarrassing. What do you say to someone who's wearing your dinner all over his shirt? "Excuse me, but may I have that back?" That's like asking for permission to do it again. Once is bad enough, but occasionally I'll be eating somewhere, and I'll make the same mess over and over. No matter how many times I try to take a bite of food, invariably it will miss my mouth. And when that happens, there's not much I can do except swallow my pride, tell a joke, and try to deflect some of the humiliation I'm feeling inside.

One food I am grateful for is mashed potatoes. From peas and carrots to corn and lima beans, mashed potatoes are the glue that holds everything together—everything on my dinner plate, that is. Mom and Dad always wondered why I mixed my food together. Everyone else took a bite of meat, a bite of vegetables, and then a bite of potato. Not me. The potatoes and the corn had to be together, and if we had gravy to put on top, so much the better. My dinner plate might look a little like the inside of a slop bucket, but I figured if that's what it took to avoid making meal-time seem like a free-for-all food fight at a high school cafeteria, then so be it.

The most frustrating thing, even with mashed potatoes, is that I never know when an accident is going to happen. I never know when I'm going to push just a little too hard and have my entire meal end up all over my neighbor's lap. It reminds me of the joke about the waitress who had cerebral palsy and was fired because none of the customers liked the way she "tossed the salad." It's never a question of whether or not I will make a mess. The only questions are when the mess will occur, and who will be sitting next to me when it happens.

In college, I had the habit of bringing a sweater with me every time I went to the cafeteria, just in case anything major went wrong during a meal. I often ended up with more food on my shirt than in my mouth, and I dreaded the idea of walking all the way back to the dormitory with a six-inch gravy stain across my chest. Whenever an accident happened, all I had to do was put that sweater on and zip it up over the stain, and nobody knew the difference. I knew, though. And although I can joke about it now, there have been times in my life when I've just wanted to crawl under the table and disappear into the carpet.

One of my earliest memories of being asked about my disability involves an incident that occurred when I was about five years old. I was outside watching Dad do some work in the yard when a neighbor boy saw us. "What's wrong with you?" he asked, noticing the trouble I had walking. He was a nice-enough kid and asked what seemed to him to be a perfectly innocent question, but it caught me off guard. I froze. I knew exactly what he was asking, but all I wanted to do was hide. "What's wrong with you?" he asked again. I forced myself to talk and mumbled something about having cerebral palsy. I managed to answer his question, but inside I was dying of embarrassment. For the first time in my life I was confronted by the fact that other people saw me as being different—as disabled. And I have spent the rest of my life hiding from that reality.

It's important to understand that for a long time I never saw myself as disabled. I always knew that I had cerebral palsy, but "having cerebral palsy" feels different from "being disabled." It's the difference between saying "I have cerebral palsy" and saying "I am disabled." Cerebral palsy is what I have; disabled is who I am. The difference may seem insignificant to some, but understanding the distinction between the two terms is crucial to understanding what it's like for me to live life with a disability. Like the car I drive or the home I live in, cerebral palsy is just one of the many aspects of my life. Being disabled, on the other hand, goes to the very root of who I am as a person. It's a label that tells people that I'm different—and possibly inferior.

I don't want to give the wrong impression. While I would rather not have to deal with the reactions of others, I am not one to stay at home, live the life of a hermit, and never venture out in public. For me, that is an unacceptable alternative to the lifestyle I've grown accustomed to. I refuse to settle for anything short of living a full and productive life as a member of my community. I'm proud of the things I've accomplished. I've put myself through four years of college, plus graduate school, and started a ministry that has already affected the lives of thousands of people. Yet, despite all of my accomplishments, I still have a sea of insecurities so deep that at times I am paralyzed by feelings of worthlessness and shame.

Two

Kitchen Chairs, Rooftops, and Pig Slime

I'm always amazed when I hear someone talk about how much courage it must have taken me to learn how to walk. I don't feel that what I did was all that courageous. There might have been some tenacity on my part, but even that is pushing it a little. It's not like I had any real choice in the matter. Mom and Dad were the ones pushing the physical therapy, not me. I wanted to walk, but I wasn't too keen on the idea of spending every night doing the same thing over and over again until I got it right.

I had to learn to do everything step-by-step, even things that most people never think about. Take falling, for instance. I fall a lot, more so when I was younger than now, although I can still take a really good tumble from time to time. You might think falling would be the one thing I wouldn't have had to learn. Don't count on it. There's a right way and a wrong way to fall, and an easy way to tell the two apart is that the wrong way hurts.

Every week I worked with one of the therapists from the local Easter Seals center. She would stand me up and tell me to lean forward with my hands out in front of me to break my fall. As soon as I hit the floor, she helped me up, gave me a pep talk, and told me to do it again. And again, and again, and again. I fell forward, then backward, then to one side, and then to the other side. The idea was to fall until I could move my hands without thinking, so that whenever I lost my balance, I could hit the ground and not hurt myself. It must have worked, because in all these years I've never broken anything. And that includes the time I almost fell off the roof.

One of the common characteristics of kids with cerebral palsy is that they're afraid of heights. It's scary enough just falling while you're on your own two feet, much less when you're standing on anything with any height to it. As a kid, I was so terrified of heights that I couldn't even sit on a kitchen chair by myself without becoming petrified that I'd fall off.

I was nine years old when Dad came up with a plan to help me overcome my fear. "How would you like to go to the roof with me?" he asked one afternoon after leaning a ladder up against the side of the house.

I wasn't too sure about the idea, but I decided to give it a try if he promised to stay close behind me and keep his arms where I could see them. I made the first step without any problems. And the second step. But by the time I stepped onto the third rung of the ladder, I was having second thoughts. I was higher than I'd ever been in my life, and I was smart enough to know that what goes up always comes down. And if I slipped, coming down would definitely hurt—something that I wanted to avoid at all cost.

"I don't know about this," I said, with more than just a little fear in my voice.

"You can't quit now," Dad said, not letting me give up.

It took ten minutes, and a lot of coaxing from Dad, for me to climb my way to the top of the ladder, but I made it. I'm glad I did. You cannot imagine how it feels to have cerebral palsy, to have been afraid of heights all your life, and then suddenly to be standing on a housetop. There's nothing like it. I felt like I was on top of the world, and from that day forward, Dad and I took regular trips to the roof together.

I was sitting on the roof one day when curiosity got the better of me. I wanted to see the ground below, so I got down on my stomach, inched my way over to the edge of the roof, and looked down. "Dad, I think I need help," I said, beginning to panic.

"What's wrong?"

"I can't get up."

"What do you mean you can't get up?"

"I think I'm going to fall!"

I hadn't thought about the fact that the roof was sloped, nor about the fact that from that position I wouldn't have strength enough to pull myself backward. I was stuck and had only one way to go—down. Fortunately, and I say that with the utmost respect for the power of gravity, Dad was close enough to come to my rescue before I could make my first and last attempt at being Superman.

I remember one time, about a year or so later, when I would have given almost anything to keep from falling. Our neighbors were pig farmers, and I loved going over to play in their fields. I was there by myself one afternoon, as I had been many times before, only this time I had a little trouble getting out of the barnyard afterward.

It had rained earlier in the week, and the ground was slippery. The only way home was through the gate, and the only way to reach the gate was through the mud. I tried everything I could think of to keep from falling. I took one step, stopped to make sure I had my balance, and then took another step. I almost made it, but not quite. I came within 6 feet of the gate before slipping, but that 6 feet might as well have been 600 feet. And before I knew it, I was down on the ground and covered from head to toe with mud and pig manure.

I pulled myself up, got to my feet, and tried again. But my second attempt at reaching the gate was no better than the first. Before I even tried to take another step, I was once again swimming in the smelliest concoction of sludge imaginable. I tried again, and again, and again, and again, but every time I tried to stand up, I fell down. And every time I fell down I got more and more soaked, until finally I gave up on the idea of walking.

I would have called for help if there had been anyone close enough to hear me. There wasn't, though, and that left only one thing to do. I had to crawl my way out, pulling myself through the mud and whatever else the animals had left there for me to bathe in. It was humiliating. Anyone else could have reached the gate in two steps, but I had to crawl on my belly through wet manure before reaching it. When I got home, Mom made me take off all my clothes before coming inside. Why not? I might as well strip naked in plain view of all the neighbors. I didn't have any dignity left anyway.

Most of the time, I can tolerate living with cerebral palsy. I don't like it, but I can tolerate it. After all, what choice do I have? But on some days, having cerebral palsy becomes almost unbearable. The day I came home soaked in pig slime was one of those days. The day I was forced to give up my crutches was another.

"Steve has done so well during the last couple of years," Dr. Suma told Mom, ignoring the fact that I was in the room and could hear everything that was said. "I think it's time for him to stop using his crutches and begin using canes."

I suppose that for most people there probably isn't much difference between the braces I wore on my legs and the crutches I used for getting around, but to me the difference was very real. Although I hated the braces and was embarrassed to be seen wearing them, a lifetime of experience told me that the only way that I could walk was with my crutches. They had allowed me to do things that I had never thought possible, and I had learned to rely on them as though my life depended on it. I was only six years old, and the thought of throwing the crutches away and trying to walk with canes sent chills down my back. I was getting along just fine and wasn't about to switch to the canes without a fight.

It's a good thing that I didn't have any choice in the matter. Although understandable, my fears were unfounded, and I made more progress in the next twelve months than at any other time in my life. After I had walked with the canes for about a year, it was time to give them up. A lot of work went into learning to walk unaided. I had to move one foot forward, regain my balance, bring the other foot forward, regain my balance again, and then repeat the process. I started out by holding onto Dad's hand, but as my coordination improved, I was eventually able to let go and begin taking steps on my own. That was the tricky part. I was okay as long as I had something to hold onto, but as soon as I let go, I landed on the floor. Falling was inevitable; the only question was of how many steps I would take before going down. Other people made it look so easy, yet here I was, taking two steps and falling flat on my face.

There are very few times in life when a person is able to look back and pinpoint a specific moment that changed his life forever. Such a moment leaves an indelible mark on your mind—one that you never forget. My life was changed the night I went from taking 10 to 15 steps at a time to taking 143 steps without falling. After all the years of going to therapy and practicing my crawling and walking at home night after night, my efforts finally paid off. It had taken me until the age of seven to do what other kids usually do as toddlers, but I was walking, and that's all that counted. I felt as though I had accomplished the impossible, and in many ways I had. I had done what many people said I would never be able to do. I had learned to walk, and for the rest of my life I will be able to look back on that night as the night I took my biggest step, both literally and figuratively. That's the night I learned to walk.

Three

Alternative Education: School for the Blind?

To continue my story, I must go back a couple of years. In the summer of 1963 I turned five, and like all other kids my age, I was old enough to begin school. When Mom called the district office to ask what had to be done in order to enroll a new student ready to enter kindergarten, a secretary on the other end of the phone assured her that there was nothing to it. "All Steve needs," she said, "is a school physical, a completed and signed registration form, and some school supplies—glue, paste, scissors, and so on."

As to whether or not any accommodations could be made in the classroom because of my cerebral palsy, that question was met with a bewildered silence. Apparently, the school district had little or no experience with physically disabled kids who demonstrated above-average intelligence, because nobody there knew what to do with me. After a few moments, one of the school's administrators came up with what seemed to her a brilliant idea. "It might be easier," she suggested, "for both Steve and the other students in the school, if he attends the school for blind children, a couple of miles from here."

I hope that today people know that something is fundamentally wrong with placing a kid with perfect vision in a school that is specifically designed for visually impaired students, even if that kid has cerebral palsy. At the time, however, their plan seemed to make sense to them. I could go to school to receive an education, yet I wouldn't disrupt the "normal" kids in school. Unfortunately, that's what it boiled down to. The school simply did not want to be bothered with accommodating a disabled student in the classroom. It was easier to ship me off somewhere else than to figure out a way to educate me at a regular school for nondisabled students.

In any event, my parents' persistence paid off, and I was mainstreamed during a time in our country when most kids with disabilities were either placed in an institution or kept at home. The Education for all Handicapped Children Act, which would guarantee disabled kids the right to a free public education in the least restrictive environment, was still a dozen years away.

For the first three years, I was one of the most popular kids in school. Whatever my classmates did, I did. From recess to nap time, from painting to learning to read, I did it all. The other kids paid little attention to the electric typewriter sitting on my desk that I used to do my class work. Nor did they seem to mind that I left class two or three days a week to go to physical therapy and to the local high school, where I learned all the ins and outs of operating a typewriter. My classmates went out of their way to accept me and made me feel that I belonged in their class. Unfortunately, everything changed when our family moved to Newark Township in southern Wisconsin in the fall of 1966.

Mom and Dad bought an old farmhouse about ten miles from town a couple of months after I began third grade. I was excited about the move and looked forward to finding the same kind of friends at my new school as I had at my old one. But to my surprise, that didn't happen. It's hard for anyone to enter a new school in the middle of the semester, but it's especially difficult when that someone has cerebral palsy. I was the outsider trying to fit into an already established group of friends. It's not that any of the kids intentionally tried to exclude me. It was simply easier for them to pretend that I did not exist and to ignore me than to make a sincere effort at friendship.

It wasn't until about a year later that the teasing started. One kid in particular went out of his way to make my life miserable. There wasn't anything nice about Bobby Hogan. Bobby and I rode the same school bus, and every day it was always the same—teasing, teasing, and more teasing. For whatever reason, he took great pleasure in watching me get mad. "Hey, Steve! Come over here!" he'd say, just to get my attention. "Is your real name Shaky?" he'd whisper as he ran away, knowing full well that I was incapable of catching him. I wanted to kill the guy. Okay, maybe that's a little extreme, but I wanted at least to hurt him just as much as he had hurt me. I would have, too, if he had stood still long enough for me to get my hands around his neck.

Bobby was the worst but by no means the only kid I had trouble with at Newark Elementary School. Jim Phillips seemed like a nice-enough kid; he was nice enough, that is, when Bobby wasn't around. But when the two of them were together, Jim became a different person, and at my expense. He was torn between trying to be my friend and wanting Bobby to like him. I asked him once why he treated me one way when we were alone and another way when Bobby was around. "I have to," he confessed, "or else Bobby won't be my friend."

His answer seemed pretty lame. How could a person be a friend one minute and not a friend the next? In Jim's defense, I have to say that he did apologize. A couple of years after graduating from high school we happened to be together, and he told me how sorry he was for some of the things he had done and said in grade school. It was good of him to apologize, even if the apology was twelve years late in coming.

I wish that Bobby and Jim had been the only two kids who tried to make my life miserable. Unfortunately, there were others as well. Dave Thompson kept to himself most of the time and usually caused little or no trouble in the classroom. But every once in awhile, when he saw me off in the corner somewhere by myself, he would get his nose out of joint and go out of his way to torment me. Such was the case one day during an afternoon recess period during the sixth grade.

Both of us had stopped off at the restroom. I was going to the bathroom, minding my own business, when Dave noticed that I had dribbled a couple of drops of urine onto the tile floor about an inch away from the base of the urinal. I noticed the look of mischief in his eyes and a few minutes later discovered what he was up to.

"Dave told me about what happened in the restroom," Mrs. Palmer said, as I walked into class. "Would you explain yourself?"

I wish I had had the courage to challenge Dave on the spot. But at eleven years of age, I lacked the courage needed to defend myself against such an outrageous accusation. Instead of standing up for myself as I should have, I just stood there and listened to Mrs. Palmer lecture me in front of 30 other students about how disappointed she was in me for having relieved myself on the middle of the restroom floor.

A couple of years later, I had another run-in with Dave, only this time we were leaving the gymnasium and heading for the guys' locker room. Dave said he wanted to play a game, the object of which was for him to run up, touch my crotch with his hand, and then run away before I could do anything about it. Some game! It may have been fun for Dave, but it wasn't fun for me. It was humiliating to have him touch me. Why would he do such a thing?

I was too embarrassed to tell anyone about the stunt Dave pulled that day, so I decided to keep the whole thing to myself—a decision I now regret. What Dave did was wrong, and someone should have set him straight about what a stupid and intrusive thing he had done.

I struggled for a long time with whether or not to write about so many of the details related above. I wasn't sure how necessary it would be to describe some of the more embarrassing things that Dave did to me over the several years that I knew him. But after giving the matter a lot of thought, I've concluded that, as humiliating as they are to write about, the things that happened between Dave Thompson and me are very important parts of my life.

If a few people are uncomfortable with reading some of the more graphic details of what happened to me in childhood, I understand that. But I want my readers to understand that it's not easy being a kid with a disability. These events provide a very real glimpse of what it was like for me growing up with cerebral palsy. Having cerebral palsy is hard. And sometimes, as was the case with knowing Dave Thompson, having cerebral palsy is down-right awful.

Four

A Place to Belong

As difficult as my last four years of grade school were for me, junior high wasn't much better. My luck in finding friends hadn't improved, and even though most of the teasing ended, the loneliness and isolation I felt only intensified.

It would not be fair of me to blame my lack of friends on my classmates alone. By the time I entered junior high, I was so starved for friendship that, in my attempt to gain the acceptance of my peers, I had become socially inept. Every school has at least one kid whom no one likes. In my school, I was that kid. I simply tried too hard to fit in and, in the process, kept turning everyone off.

On the other hand, high school opened up a whole new world for me. It all started the day Mark Campbell and Jim and Alvin Hammill came up to me during lunch. "Hey, Steve," one of them said, "we're having a Youth for Christ meeting tonight at Mike McMahon's apartment. Would you like to come?"

"I'm not sure."

"It's just down the road," someone said, offering me a ride.

As I walked through the front door of Mike's apartment later that evening, I was greeted by twenty students jammed into the living room of a small apartment. They were getting ready for the start of their annual "wacky auction." Everyone had rummaged through his or her bedroom closet and found the most worthless items possible, including old tennis shoes and half-used rolls of toilet paper, and had brought them to be auctioned off to the highest bidder. And bid they did! I couldn't believe how much people paid. Someone had brought an old corn cob, and even that brought 10 cents.

I left the meeting that night glad that I had decided to go. Although I didn't realize it then, that meeting was a real turning point in my life. I came back the next week, the week after that, and the week after that. I kept coming back for the next four years, until it was time to leave for college. Youth for Christ was important to me. It provided a place where I could go and connect with people. I was a somebody again, with friends to spend time with instead of always staying home and feeling sorry for myself, wondering if life would ever improve.

I had become a Christian a few years earlier and will discuss my conversion in a later chapter. However, I had never experienced spiritual growth or Christian fellowship until I joined YFC. God used that ministry to change my life, both spiritually and socially. By the time I was a junior, it was a popular thing to be a friend of Steve Chance. I am not bragging about how well liked I was in high school. Just the opposite. I am deeply humbled by how God has worked in my life, especially during those awkward, growing-up years.

I am well aware that if it weren't for the three guys who brought me to my first club meeting, my life might have gone in a totally different direction. What amazes me about my involvement with Youth for Christ is how ready I was to belong to something. It would have probably made no difference what kind of group I joined, just as long as the people in that group wanted me there. It could have been the Hare Krishnas, the Moonies, or even someone like Jim Jones down in South America, inviting me to drink red Kool-Aid. It just happened that the three guys who invited me to my first youth meeting were Christians, and for that I will be eternally grateful.

Some of my fondest memories are of my experiences in Youth for Christ. The club went on a lot of camping trips, and every

February at least fifty kids went into northern Wisconsin for what they called their "Sno-Ball Weekend." The bus left the parking lot around 7 P.M. Thursday night and pulled into camp sometime after midnight. From then until Sunday afternoon we played in the snow, attended seminars, and chowed down on camp food. Some of us even managed to get a few hours of shut-eye, starting around 2:00 or 3:00 in the morning.

What I remember most about the Sno-Ball trips is the ski slope. It wasn't nearly as big as some of the slopes I've seen in other parts of the country since then, but it was big enough so that I knew I had to try going down it at least once. I started out on the "bunny hill" with the other beginners and spent most of the time lying in a snowbank, trying to figure out how to stand up without taking off my skis. I was okay as long as I was standing, but I did not have the strength or the coordination to get on my feet after falling. I lasted for about an hour; after that I was just too exhausted to keep going. I hadn't broken any bones, and for the rest of my life I could tell people about the time that I skied Rib Mountain during winter camp.

As much as I liked the idea of being able to ski, that's how much I hated the inner-tube run. It started three-fourths of the way up the side of the mountain and extended across the lake. A person could top 50 miles an hour by the time he reached the bottom if he did it right. I've experienced real fear only a few times in my life, and one of those times was while riding an inner-tube down that mountain. I was prepared for the speed, but no one had mentioned that you bounce all over the place on the way down. I finished my run halfway across the lake and decided that once was enough. I spent the rest of the afternoon in the lodge with all the staff and other campers who would rather sit around the fire, drinking hot chocolate and talking, than to brave the sub-zero temperatures outside.

The only time I remember actually being angry at somebody at YFC, at least while I was in high school, was during a 20-mile walkathon held to raise money for the program. I worked my tail off to raise almost $200 in pledges, which was enough to earn a $25 prize for being one of the group's top fund-raisers. Because I thought it might be easier than walking from Beloit to Orfordville,

I opted to ride my 26-inch, three-wheel bike instead. I arrived at the YFC office a little early and turned in my pledge sheet and all the money I had collected. A few minutes later I jumped on my bike, and twenty of us headed for the edge of town for what I thought would be a long and exhausting day of riding. Shortly after that, Dick Myers, director of the program, told me he had some bad news.

"I just spoke with someone from the sheriff's office who said that you can't take your bike along the main road to Orfordville."

"Why?"

"It's not safe."

"What do you mean, it's not safe?"

"He said that with three wheels, your bike is too wide for the main road."

"This trip has been planned for a couple of months!" I shouted. "You knew that I planned on riding my bike to Orford-ville. Why did you wait until the day of the trip to tell me this?"

After arguing for another ten minutes, I finally resigned myself to walking. "I'm afraid you can't do that either," Dick admitted.

"Why?"

"Because you might hurt yourself."

"No, I won't!"

"We can't take that chance."

"Says who?" I retorted.

I was mad! Yet despite my protest, Dick told me to get off the bike and into the van. I had spent weeks raising money for their program, and now they wanted me to sit in a van and watch everyone else walk. I understood that he couldn't do anything about the bike, but he had no right to stop me from walking. If he was concerned about my keeping up with the group, he should have called my parents and talked to them. Both were at home and would gladly have laid to rest any fears about my walking such a long distance. Instead, he took it upon himself to decide arbitrarily what I could and could not do and humiliated me in the process. To make matters worse, he still wanted me to collect my pledge money and even suggested that I tell people that the few miles I rode counted for the twenty miles everyone else walked.

Dick knew I was upset and called later that evening. I have forgotten exactly what he said to make amends, but I made certain that he knew never to humiliate me like that again—not if he wanted me to be involved in YFC. Dick wouldn't agree to doing another walkathon, as I asked, but he did promise to put together a bike trip for later that summer. I had something to prove, and he owed me the chance to prove it.

Dick kept his word, and one Saturday a few months later several of us set out on a thirty-mile bike ride. I was such a glutton for punishment back then. The first half of the trip was pretty easy, and I felt good when we stopped at the bottom of a long, steep hill for lunch. I loved riding my bike, and going downhill was the best part. There's nothing like spending twenty minutes going uphill in first gear, pedaling your heart out, and then turning around and flying back down as fast as you can, with nothing to stop you but a stop sign at the next crossroad a mile away. Going downhill first is just not the same. It's like eating a pint of ice cream and then having lima beans afterwards. I can do it, but what's the fun of eating lima beans for dessert?

We ate a couple of hamburgers, played a few games, and mounted up for the trip home. At least, some of the group got on their bikes. Others of us swallowed our pride, pushed our bikes to the top, and then got back on them for the long ride home. By the time we arrived back in Orfordville, I thought I was going to die. My legs felt like rubber, my arms were about to fall off, and every muscle in my body ached from fatigue. Did I care? Not on your life! I couldn't remember a time when I had felt better. I had done what I had set out to do. I had ridden thirty miles in a single day, and no one had told me to get into a van or said that I was going too slow for the rest of the group. The fact is, most of the time I was ahead of somebody, and usually that somebody was Dick Myers. Even after all these years, it feels good to remember that he had to work just as hard as I did to finish the trip.

I proved something to the people who were with me that day—something that, even at age 16, I had already known for a long time. I proved that I am capable of achieving much more in life than most people think possible. That's not to say that I'm capable of doing anything I want merely because I put my mind to it. I have a fairly realistic view of my limitations. I will never run in the Olympics, become a brain surgeon, or give a piano concert at Carnegie Hall. Those things are not only out of the question for me, but they are also out of the realm of possibility for a lot of other energetic and ambitious people, many of whom do not have disabilities.

What it all boils down to is this: Although I'm well aware that I cannot do certain things in life because of my cerebral palsy, I also know that I can do many other things, if only I'm given the chance to try. I know that I'm going to fail at some things, and that's okay. The only people who never fail are people without goals, and I definitely have goals for my life. However, my ambitions are my business. No one has the right to decide what I can try to do but me.

Five

Healing: Asking the Tough Questions

"God wants to do a miracle in your life! Turn to Jesus and be healed!" I was four years old when I started watching Oral Roberts on television. On his early morning program, he invited one person after another to join him on stage, where he prayed with each of them for healing. I watched in awe as he laid his hands on the person's head, closed his eyes, and pleaded for God to reach down and perform a miracle. I couldn't believe what I was seeing. Blind people began to see, deaf people began to hear, and people in wheelchairs began to walk. Then, at the end of each service, Oral looked straight into the camera and invited sick and disabled television viewers to pray with him. "God loves you," Oral said. "God loves you and wants to do miracles for you. All you have to do is believe, today, and God will hear your prayers and heal your body."

That's what I wanted. I wanted a miracle. I wanted God to heal me the same way he healed those people Oral prayed for on television. I believed Oral, and when he prayed, I prayed. I was sure that God heard my prayers and that it was only a matter of time before he completely took away my cerebral palsy.

Oral Roberts used to have a tent ministry, and he went from one town to another holding healing crusades. Thousands of people came to hear him speak and see him perform the miracles for which he was famous. Soon after I began watching his television program, he came to our area, and Dad asked me if I wanted to see Oral in person. You must realize that Oral Roberts seemed like God to me, and having him pray for me would be like having Jesus himself lay his hands on me. "Yes! I want to go!" I said. I wanted Oral to reach out his hands, touch my body, and pray for God to heal me. It was only a matter of time, I thought, before I could throw away my crutches, take off my braces, and walk like everyone else.

Things didn't happen that way, however. I went to the crusade, fully expecting God to heal me, but was kept from seeing Oral for all but the last few minutes of the meeting. My parents and I spent most of the night with a group of other disabled people listening to someone from his staff talk about how we should give money to the ministry. I don't remember many of the details, but I imagine that the presentation included something about how a donation could be the key to unleashing the faith required to receive a miracle. It must have sounded so inviting. God could do anything, and the only thing required for a five-year-old boy to be healed of cerebral palsy was a little faith, demonstrated by the size of his parents' check written to the ministry.

It didn't matter to me that we were kept segregated from everyone in the main auditorium or that I saw Oral for only a few seconds. I was on cloud nine that night, and before we left the parking lot, I was sure that God had healed me. Maybe I still had a little trouble walking, but that seemed so insignificant compared to the fact that Oral Roberts had just prayed for me. I was certain that by the time I went to bed and woke up again the next morning, my cerebral palsy would be gone.

Over the course of the next several days, reality set in, and that's when I began accepting the fact that God had not healed me. I was disappointed and unsure of what to think. If a man like Oral Roberts could not talk God into healing me, I felt that I had no chance of asking God for myself.

That night was never mentioned much around our house. The only thing that changed was that we stopped going to church. The church that we attended closed its doors for lack of support, and after that, we just never found anywhere else to attend.

For the next few years, I didn't know how I felt about God. I had once believed that God was real, but I had also believed in miracles. Maybe the whole thing was make-believe, and God was like Santa Claus or the Easter Bunny. Perhaps he was good enough for kids to believe in, but by the time a person becomes an adult, he or she was better off letting go of childhood fantasies.

My doubts about God continued until the spring of 1970. That's when Mom began taking us to the Avon Community Church, located just a few miles south of the little town of Brodhead. Avon is an independent church about the size of a one-room schoolhouse and, at the time, was heated with an oil-burning space heater. It also had no inside plumbing, and people either used their own bathrooms before they left home or used the two-seater outhouse located behind the church. On a good morning, there might be twenty people at the service, including any visitors who happened to stop by. The church paid Ralph Wilson, an older, semi-retired man who ran a Christian bookstore in Janesville, $35 a week to be their pastor.

About a month after we started attending the services at Avon, I was sitting next to Mom, waiting for church to be over, when something happened that changed my life forever. When it came time to sing the last hymn, instead of asking the congregation to open their hymnals, Pastor Wilson invited us to make our way to the front of the church for communion.

"Do you believe in God?" he asked, pausing a moment for emphasis.

At first I thought the question was rhetorical, but I soon discovered otherwise. Pastor Wilson looked directly at me and made it pretty clear that he expected me to answer, audibly, and in front of everyone.

"Me?" I asked sheepishly.

"Yes," he said, nodding his head.

What did I know about God? I was eleven years old at the time and wasn't sure what I believed. The way I looked at the situation, I could do one of two things. I could be honest and say that I didn't believe in God. Or I could lie. I figured that I would surprise a lot of people if I told the truth. I was in church, after all, and people who went to church were supposed to believe in God. Besides, if God really did exist, I knew I would be in major trouble down the road if I publicly denied him now.

I decided to play it safe. "Yes," I told Pastor Wilson and everyone else listening. "I believe. I believe that God is real." Before the words were out of my mouth, I knew that something had changed inside of me. Every doubt I ever had left me. I might not have been able to explain to people why I had cerebral palsy or to answer many other questions about God's sovereignty, but as soon as I spoke, I knew that God existed, that he loved me, and that he wanted to be an integral part of my life.

After going through most of grade school feeling cut off from my classmates, the realization that Christ was seeking an intimate relationship with me was absolutely overwhelming. I had gone from being disliked by some and ignored by others to being loved by the living God. There is no way for me to adequately describe the acceptance I felt from this God who loves me despite my disability. I didn't have to prove myself to God. His love is total and complete, and isn't something I had to earn. He loves me, Steve Chance, cerebral palsy and all. Let me tell you, that level of acceptance after years and years of rejection from classmates was incredibly refreshing.

It wasn't until several years later, after joining Youth for Christ, that I began to understand the significance of that morning. What started out as a safe answer had turned into an open acknowledgment of my belief in Jesus Christ. I had become a Christian. And by attending Youth for Christ club meetings and Bible studies during high school, my commitment to Jesus Christ grew.

The flip side to all of this is that along with my new faith in Christ came a renewed interest in healing. You might think that, after what had occurred at the Oral Roberts crusade years earlier, I would have learned my lesson. Yet, I desperately wanted to believe the things that some of my high school friends were telling me. "God is alive," they concluded. "If Christ did miracles 2000 years ago, he can do them today. All you have to do is ask." I believed what they said. For the second time in my life, I asked God to give me a body that did not shake with cerebral palsy.

What would my life really be like without cerebral palsy? I don't know. Some of the benefits would be obvious, such as being able to hold a glass of water without spilling any of it or eating a complete meal without making a mess. Yet cerebral palsy is so much a part of who I am that I can't imagine what life would be like without it. I was more than willing to find out, though.

Some people might wonder why I again asked God to heal me. I have asked myself that same question over and over again, and I always return to the same two answers. The first is that I wanted so much to be seen as just another person that I clung to any hope at all that one day I might not have to deal with cerebral palsy. When all is said and done, life would simply be much easier without a disability.

The second reason I so desperately wanted to be healed was because I thought that was the way God could best use me. Imagine, a lifetime of cerebral palsy swept away with one prayer. What a testimony! No one could deny the reality of a God who does miracles. That's what I wanted—to be a living, breathing, and walking testimony for the God who takes away cerebral palsy.

Life did not work out that way, though, and after some time had passed, I found myself asking some pretty hard questions about why I wasn't being healed. I thought that I must have somehow failed. Perhaps I had neglected to confess some hidden sin in my life or failed to find the right formula to unleash God's supernatural power. Either way, I saw myself as an embarrassment to the church, especially to churchgoers who had encouraged me to continue praying for healing.

Looking back, I realize that I had caused a bit of theological confusion among some of my well-meaning Christian friends. They thought they had God all figured out and were convinced that if I prayed hard enough and believed long enough, God was bound to answer my prayers. But God didn't answer, at least not in the way my friends intended. Instead, for whatever reason, God chose to remain silent. And with that silence came a host of questions accompanied by the guilt and shame of once again not measuring up to other people's expectations.

I have heard many sermons on the subject of healing since becoming an adult, and most pastors are somewhere on a continuum between two extremes. On one end, some deny God's willingness to heal. They are convinced that the age of miracles ended with the death of the apostles, and they frown on any mention of supernatural healing. Any attempt to pray for physical healing is considered by them a waste of time and something that should be discouraged.

Though this approach might sound reasonable to some people, it seems a little too unyielding for me. I can't bring myself to say that God never heals, because I believe that he does. On the other hand, I'm equally uncomfortable with pastors at the other end of the spectrum who believe that God always answers the prayers of the faithful in the way that they demand. They insist that sickness is never God's will, that the Bible says as much, and that God will wait until you can muster up enough faith to unleash his healing power.

From my perspective, both extremes are dangerous because they both undermine the working of God. The first fails to acknowledge any divine intervention that falls outside the realm of nature, and the second denies the reality that God can and will work through persons who suffer. Unfortunately, it's the second extreme that has caused me the most heartache.

Although I've come to terms with the fact that God has not answered my plea for a miracle, some in the Christian community are still intent on seeing me healed. I was in a drugstore recently, buying a newspaper and a couple of batteries, when a man wearing a huge metallic cross approached me. He tried to engage me in a conversation about God being a healing God and, when I wouldn't bite, proceeded to pray for me right there in front of the other customers. Granted, most Christians are not this extreme or radical in demonstrating their beliefs. But this example does illustrate how disabled people are often viewed as broken objects needing to be fixed, instead of as people capable of entering into meaningful relationships.

I want to be careful not to be misunderstood. I am not suggesting that God cannot or will not heal. Nor am I suggesting that we not ask God to heal our physical bodies. My concern has more to do with well-meaning Christians who focus on my disability to the exclusion of me as a person. That was not the ministry of Jesus Christ, and that should not be the ministry of the church today. What should we tell people who have prayed all of their lives for God to bring healing to their bodies? That they don't have enough faith? That there is sin in their lives? Or should we assure them that God is faithful and hasn't abandoned them— that where they hurt, God hurts, and in that hurt God stands ready to meet them?

I wish someone had given me that message when I was in high school, or in college, or at any other time in my life when I needed to hear that I did not have to prove myself to God. As it was, God's faithfulness and grace are concepts that I had to figure out for myself.

Six

Driving: A Badge of Normalcy

Like a lot of teenagers, I had my first driving lesson a few months before my sixteenth birthday. Dad had an old '64 Chevy that had a manual transmission with the gearshift located on the steering column. He took me out to the driveway one afternoon and told me to get behind the steering wheel. I started the engine, shifted into reverse, let the clutch out, and almost wrecked the car by backing into a tree. Ouch! I missed the tree, but I think Dad may have had second thoughts about my getting behind the wheel. I know my neighbor did. Her car was parked in the driveway, only a few feet away from the tree that I almost demolished. She rushed out of her house and moved the car onto the street. I don't know what she was afraid of. I'd been driving for a good three minutes by the time she came out, and I hadn't had even one accident in all that time. Near misses don't count.

I had always assumed that I'd be able to drive. Why not? I had always done everything else I wanted to do. Why should driving be any different? All I had to do was get my driving permit, take driver's ed., and pass the road test. Nothing to it, right? Believe it or not, it was almost that simple. I think I had to get my doctor's okay to get a permit, but once I learned to stay away from trees, everything else came easy.

I had trouble with two things on the day of the test: backing up and giving hand signals. I paid more attention to how I held the steering wheel than to the direction in which the car was headed. I knew how to back up. But I was so busy showing the examiner that I knew how to drive, I didn't even think about where I was going.

As for the signaling, that's another story. The examiner asked me to give a right hand signal. Because my window was shut (and because I have more control in my right hand than I do in my left), I stopped the car, rolled down the window with my right hand, started driving again, and then proceeded to give the appropriate hand signal. That's not the kind of thing that most people do while taking the road test. Yet I couldn't give a signal with the window closed, and opening it with my left hand might have been disastrous. The examiner questioned me afterward about stopping the car but then went ahead and passed me anyway. He must have figured that if I was cautious enough to avoid doing something I deemed unsafe during a road test, I would probably make a good driver. That was only a few weeks after my sixteenth birthday, and I've been driving ever since.

Other people may take their driver's licenses for granted. Not me. I'm well aware of the fact that if I had been born just a little more disabled, I wouldn't be able to drive. Even with the control that I do have in my arms and legs, I've still had my license questioned on numerous occasions. Every time I go to the Department of Motor Vehicles, I know ahead of time what to expect—questions about my disability. It never fails. No matter how good a driver I've been, my cerebral palsy always becomes an issue.

I never will forget the time when the guy behind the desk at the DMV looked at me and asked, "What seems to be the problem?" What kind of a question is that, anyway? I didn't have a problem. I may have had cerebral palsy, but I didn't have a problem.

Now, I don't want to indict all the DMV employees in the country. They're only doing their jobs, and I understand that. If I were in their shoes and saw me coming through the door, I'd question my ability to drive, too. However, having said that, I also want it known how much I dislike going to the DMV. It's more than just the inconvenience of answering a few questions about my disability. I hate everything about it. I hate the lines, I hate the questions, and I hate the road tests. But above all, I hate having to prove myself to the state just because of my disability. That's what it comes down to—being forced to prove myself over and over again to people who wouldn't even know my name if they didn't happen to have a government job.

I grow tired of constantly being confronted by people who make an issue of my disability, not only at the DMV, but everywhere. The only difference between the people at the DMV and every other person who questions my competency is that I can ignore everyone else. I can't do that with the state. I can't just refuse to show up at the DMV when it's time to renew my license—not if I want to go on driving legally.

For me, my driver's license is much more than just a piece of paper from the state acknowledging the fact that I am capable of operating a motor vehicle. It provides me with a freedom that I wouldn't otherwise have. It enables me to do the things that are important to me without having to rely on other people for transportation. If I want to go out for a hamburger on the spur of the moment, I can. If I want to take an afternoon off and drive to the beach for a few hours of fresh air and sunshine, I can. And if I want to visit a friend or go to a movie, I can do that, too. Driving gives me the freedom to do what I want to do, when I want to do it.

Like just about everyone else, I like my independence. But for me, knowing that the state has the power to take some of that freedom away just because I have cerebral palsy is very frightening. Every time I go to the DMV and wait for my turn in line, my whole way of life is at stake. With one failed driving test, my independence, something that I've worked for all my life, could be taken away from me. That scares me. I know that there are millions of people in this country who, for one reason or another, are unable to drive. And I also know that most of those people lead very productive and rewarding lives. But the prospect of someday losing my license is something that frightens me in a way that not much else does.

Part of me is ashamed of my anxiety about losing my license. I feel that I ought to be able to snap my fingers, trust God for the future, and not worry about whether the day might come when I will lose my independence. Perhaps I ought to be able to do that, but I can't—at least not yet. No matter how old I get, or how many years of driving experience I put behind me, the fear of losing my independence is something that never leaves me.

Why is driving so important to me? When I first began writing this chapter, I believed that the reason I place so much importance on having my license is the independence it brings me. But now that I have had a chance to reflect more about it, I'm not so sure that's true. I think that my fears have more to do with my pursuit of normalcy than with anything else. I want to be normal. I want people to look at me as they would at any other person and see past my disability to the real person inside. No, that's not quite it, either. What I really want is for people not to see the disability. I wish that I could go through life as almost everyone else does and not have to deal with being different. But, of course, that's impossible, isn't it? Because no matter how much I want my cerebral palsy to vanish, it's always with me. And although I live a very active and productive life, I also live with the constant fear of being exposed for who I really am, a man disabled with cerebral palsy.

There it is again. That awful "D" word. That's why I hate going to the DMV so much. The person who has the job of renewing my license has also been given the responsibility of deciding whether or not I will keep my license. And that decision is based, at least in part, on an examination of my disability.

I don't like being required to have my disability looked at by people I don't know. The whole experience forces me to take a closer look at myself. And the bottom line is that I don't like what I see. I don't like being disabled. Every time I go to the DMV to renew my license, I'm forced to acknowledge that I, Steven Gene Chance, am disabled. And I resent it.

Over the years, many friends have told me that they don't notice my disability. They used to notice, they say, but now that they know me, they see only the real me. The implication, of course, is that my disability isn't the real me. My personality is the real me, and my cerebral palsied body is only a superfluous appendage that should be overlooked in order to get at the real person inside.

I know they mean well, but sometimes people can do more harm than good by what they say. Cerebral palsy, disability, whatever you choose to call it—that's the real me. It may not be all of me, but it is at least part of me. To pretend otherwise is to ignore the obvious. Like it or not, I am disabled.

The hard part is living with the reality of cerebral palsy. Life would be much easier if that reality didn't exist. But because it does exist, I do the next best thing by living behind a facade of normalcy. That way I don't have to deal with all the garbage that comes with being disabled. Except, of course, when my disability is brought to my attention. And no one does that better than the folks at the DMV.

There may be some who will argue that, as a Christian, I should recognize my value to God and live my life accordingly. Although that may be true, it is easier said than done. I know that my worth comes from God, and I am profoundly grateful for what he's done in my life. However, what I'm talking about here has more to do with how I see myself than it does with whether or not I am valued by God. My value to God is a given. It's my perception that's clouded, not my actual worth. I have a lifetime of experiences telling me that no matter what I do, I'll never measure up to the expectations of others. Somewhere along the line, a part of me has come to believe that those perceptions of others about me are true, that I really am as inadequate as some people seem to think.

Seven

Taylor University: Class of 1980

One of the greatest gifts that the Youth for Christ staff gave me was to expose me to the world of higher education. Grades were never pushed much in our house. If my brother, Bill, and I came home with "C's," that was good enough for my parents. Although they were proud of the occasional "A" that we made, Mom and Dad never insisted that we make the honor roll. They figured that if we learned reading, writing, and mathematics, that was enough. It wasn't until high school that I started working for grades, and even then I never applied myself like I know I could have.

Lynn Myers, wife of YFC's executive director Dick Myers, is the one who first encouraged me to think about college. "College is completely different from high school," she told me one night after a Youth for Christ meeting. "The years I spent at Taylor University were some of the best of my life. How would you like to see the campus?"

"Sure!" I replied, uncertain of what I was getting myself into.

The first thing that caught my attention about Taylor was that the school is in the middle of nowhere. The campus sits at the edge of Upland, a town of about 2000 people, located an hour north of Indianapolis. I was impressed by Taylor. I had been a

Christian for several years and knew that I wanted to be involved somehow in ministry. The idea of spending four years at a school where I could pursue some type of biblical training excited me.

Lynn was right. The years I spent at Taylor were some of the best years of my life. I lived in Sammy Morris Hall in room 106, right across the hall from the bathroom, for three years, until I moved into Hill House during my senior year. Living in the dorm is an experience unlike any other, one that I would highly recommend to anyone wanting a thorough education. Not everything can be learned from books; some of my best memories of school are of spending time with the guys on First Morris, my floor.

First Morris wasn't exactly known for throwing wild parties. That honor went to Third West Wengatz. I thought that the only reason that someone went to college was to study. Boy, was I wrong! Those guys at Wengatz once threw a refrigerator out of a window. As if that wasn't enough, then they lit a firecracker just to see if they could blow their dorm phone off the wall. We at Morris might have participated in our share of pranks over the years, but we did nothing quite that destructive.

Bruce Smith held the honors for being the most self-disciplined. Bruce always had a book in his hand, and the 4.0 grade-point average that he had going into his senior year was proof of his diligence. I remember his saying something about wanting to get a "B" in one of his classes just to bring his GPA down to a 3.9. He hoped to be a teacher and was afraid that his grades might work against him, that he would be perceived as too unsociable.

Unlike Bruce, most of us were just your average run-of-the-mill students who attended Taylor to get a good education and to have a good time in the process. Take Greg, my first roommate, for instance. Greg was a business major from New Jersey who was more famous for his snoring than for his expertise in microeconomics. Living with Greg was like living next to a train station and having freight cars pass by all night long.

"Greg," I whispered, trying to be quiet enough so as not to wake him but loud enough to cause him to roll over. "Greg," I said again, only this time in a much more determined tone of voice. Finally, after ten minutes went by without any sign of relief, I started yelling "Greg! Greg!" loud enough to wake the guys in the room next to ours.

My screaming never did any good, though. Nothing could wake Greg. When his snoring became too unbearable, the best I could hope for was an empty lounge at the end of the hall, where I could bring a pillow and blanket and try to grab a few hours of peaceful shut-eye before breakfast. It was either that or spend the night counting an endless number of sheep to the rhythm of a high-performance chain saw. I opted for the sleep and left the neighbors to deal with Greg's high-intensity guttural noises.

One year we had our own jogging club, which started out with a couple of roommates taking a run before bedtime. This ritual soon escalated to include half the guys on the floor. Every night around 10 o'clock, they put on their sweat pants and headed outside to run along the side of the road that encircled the campus. I went along too, although the chances of my keeping up with ten guys out for a mile run were next to none. So I took the easy way out and followed on my bike. We were quite a sight—ten students jogging late at night, chased by a guy with cerebral palsy riding a three-wheel bike.

I almost didn't bring my bike to Taylor. That would have been a big mistake, since it was nearly half a mile between the dormitory and the cafeteria. Multiply that distance by three meals a day and add the distance to attend classes and then visit friends at the end of the day, and you can understand why it didn't take me long to get used to being the only one on campus riding an overgrown tricycle.

Bikes may be great for getting around when it's warm outside, but they're not made for cold weather. And neither am I. Have you ever watched someone with cerebral palsy trying to get around on ice? It's not a pretty sight. I can't remember how many times I fell in a snowbank and got soaking wet right before class. It's embarrassing to walk in with wet pants, but what's the alternative? If I had gone back to the dorm every time I slipped on a patch of ice, I would never have made it through the first year.

The good thing about having to get around on snow and ice was that people were always helpful. And sometimes, if a fall was timed just right, some girl would be walking by and offer her arm for me to hang onto. If that doesn't sound like the perfect setup for advancing my social life, I don't know what is! On more than one occasion I had to fight the temptation to take an intentional spill right in front of a good-looking girl. I never actually succumbed to the idea, but I thought about it many times. I guess I've always figured that there is just something inherently wrong about using my cerebral palsy in such a manipulative way. But I so often fell unintentionally that I really didn't need to go around falling on purpose, not even for the sake of my raging hormones!

The school rented a golf cart to help me get around better during the winter months. That may sound great, and I had my share of fun with it, but you must remember that it gets cold in Indiana during the winter. I froze my tail off riding that thing. During the first January that I was at Taylor, the wind-chill factor hit minus 85 degrees. I don't care how many clothes a person puts on—that's cold!

I had a lot of fun with that cart, except for the time I crashed while riding in the rain, on my way to the Dining Commons. The first thing I did was walk back to the dorm and knock on my residence director's door. "Lowell, I have some bad news," I said, with a look of fear written on my face.

"What happened?"

"I was trying to keep my head down so I could stay a little dry, and I hit a lamppost," I confessed, still covered with mud. "I went one way, my books went another, and I'm afraid the golf cart is wrecked."

Lowell said that he would take care of the cart and not to worry. I needed that reassurance. I didn't have much dignity left at that point, and I was sure I was in for an old-fashioned lecture about speeding in the rain. But by lunch time, whoever worked on the cart had it all fixed up and ready to go again.

I have a lot of good memories of my days at Taylor, including the time Dave Barber and Dave Henderson took me skitching out behind Pigland, a couple of miles away from campus. What's "skitching"? What's Pigland? Pigland was the name given to a nearby hog farm where pigs came right up onto the front porch of the farmhouse. It was known as the dirtiest, smelliest, and ugliest place in the county. "Skitching," on the other hand, was the name given to the fine art of holding onto the back bumper of a moving car while sliding down a snow-covered road. I had my doubts, but hey, I'll try anything once.

We drove to Pigland one morning before the county equipment had a chance to plow the road. Someone tied a piece of twine to the back bumper for me to hang on to and gave me a piece of cardboard to sit on. Henderson jumped behind the wheel, and off we went, the other guys hanging onto the bumper and me sliding on my rear end. We went from one end of that road to the other, turned around, and skitched our way back. We were out there for a couple of hours and didn't see more than two cars go by. A good thing, too, because skitching is slightly illegal in the state of Indiana. It's dangerous, especially for a person sitting on cardboard! I had no brakes, and whenever the car slowed down I had to make sure that I steered clear of the back bumper. Otherwise I might have been pulling my teeth out of Dave's license plate, and I have a real aversion to pain. I had no intention of making a trip to the emergency room and explaining how I got my teeth knocked out while playing in snow.

The month that I spent in Israel was by far the highlight of my college experience. Fifty of us boarded a plane in Chicago and headed for Tel Aviv for what turned out to be the best trip of my life. While friends back home were experiencing the worst winter to hit the midwest in 100 years, we were basking in the desert sunshine and swimming in the waters of the Dead Sea.

Our journey started with a six-day stint in Jerusalem, followed by three weeks of touring the rest of the country. From the Jordan River on the east to the Mediterranean Sea on the west, from the borders of Lebanon to the north to the tip of the Red Sea to the south, we traveled from one end of Israel to the other. A typical day started around 6:30, and by 8:00 we had dressed, packed, eaten, and were on the road for a long and grueling day of sight-seeing. We walked everywhere, stopping only long enough to take bathroom breaks and to eat lunch. By around 5:00, we usually reached whichever youth hostel we were staying at that night and had from then until 7:30 to rest, prepare our evening meal, eat, and clean up. At 7:30 we had group devotions, followed by two hours of classes starting at 8:00. By the time 10:00 came around, everyone was exhausted and ready to go to bed for a few hours of shut-eye before doing it all again the next day.

If our schedule sounds demanding, that's because it was. In fact, it was so demanding that there had been a question of whether or not I would be permitted to go on the trip. No one with cerebral palsy had ever gone before, and the staff were unsure of whether of not I could handle the grueling pace. Chuck Newman, the man organizing the trip, talked with my parents, and after watching me walk three to five miles every day in preparation for the trip, decided that I could go.

My ability to keep up was questioned only a couple of times during the course of the trip, and then the issues had more to do with safety than with endurance. One such occasion was at the foot of the stairs leading to the top of the wall surrounding the old city of Jerusalem. Chuck was afraid that I wouldn't have the balance needed to navigate the narrow ledge at the top of the stairs without falling. I must admit that his concerns were legitimate. Someone had built a railing along the initial part of the walkway, but for some reason, had left much of the ledge unrailed. Chuck agreed to let me go part-way and said that I could turn back later if I needed to. That sounded like a fair compromise, and with Chuck's okay, I climbed to the top with everyone else and started walking along the edge of the wall. I reached the point where the railing ended, looked down at the ground thirty feet below, knew that I had no business walking on a three-foot ledge that high off the ground, and promptly turned around.

I love to climb, and as long as I have something sturdy to hang onto, I'll climb anything. That's why I was so anxious to climb to the top of Masada. For those who may be unfamiliar with Jewish history, Masada is an ancient fortress that rises 1700 feet above the Dead Sea. There are two ways to get to the top. The easy way is to ride the tram. The hard way is to climb, step by step, the long, windy path that leads up the face of the mountain. I chose the hard way, not to anyone's surprise. With Jim Snyder's arm as support, it took me an hour to do what everyone else had done in 20 minutes. I made it, though. And the feelings that rushed through me as I reached the end of the trail were indescribable. Not only had I reached the top, but I had made it there under the power of my own two feet.

I enjoyed my college years, and some of my best friendships in life are those I made while at Taylor. I even got the chance to do some studying on the side. Maybe not as much as I should have, but I did study. Looking back on it, I guess my grades could have been a little better if only I had applied myself more. At the time, though, I was too busy hanging out with the guys on the floor and the girls across campus to worry about academics.

If I had known then what I know now, I would have paid more attention to grades and gone to graduate school right out of college. But back then I didn't even know what grad school was, much less how to get there. It never dawned on me that every one of my professors had advanced degrees and that those degrees had to come from somewhere. Keep in mind that my family was strictly blue collar; to the best of my knowledge, none of my relatives had ever received a bachelor's degree before I did, much less a master's or a doctorate. I was breaking new ground by going to Taylor. I was the first in my family to make it through four years of college, an accomplishment that I'm still proud of today.

Eight

Cerebral Palsy, Straws,
and a Five-Year-Old Brunette

Of all the areas of my life that cerebral palsy has touched, none has been so deeply affected by feelings of insecurity as my relationships with members of the opposite sex. Ever since I can remember, I've liked girls. Even at the ripe old age of five, I had my eyes on the prettiest girl in class. Kim Talbert sat across from me at the next table in kindergarten. She had long brown hair and was the prettiest girl I had ever met. I melted every time she looked at me, and if a kid that young can experience love at first sight, then I was in love. During the next couple of years, Kim and I became the best of friends, and we stayed that way until she moved out of town sometime during the middle of the second grade.

I've regretted losing contact with Kim more than with any other person in my life. The last I knew, she was living in Rockford, Illinois with her parents and going to grade school, but that was close to a lifetime ago. When I look back over my life, I still miss Kim. She was a special friend and someone I will never forget. Kim, wherever you are, I love you and wish you all the best that life has to offer.

Those years were truly some of the best—not just because I knew Kim, but also because of everything else going on in my life.

Every night, I was able to do things that I had never done before. My coordination was improving, my speech was getting better, and there seemed to be no limit to what I could accomplish. No limit, that is, until it came to learning to drink without using a straw. Although this seemed to be the next logical step for me to take on my way to independence, no matter how hard I tried, I could never raise a glass to my lips without spilling its entire contents all over the place. All I had to do was think about holding a glass, and every muscle in my body would tighten up and begin to shake.

Mom and Dad tried everything to keep me motivated. Every time we sat down to the dinner table I'd ask for a straw, and every time I was told to start without one. I tried. Oh, how I tried. I first used one hand and then both hands. I used one hand to hold the other hand. I even wore weights around my wrists, thinking that the added resistance would help steady the shaking. Nothing worked.

My parents were desperate. I had done so well with everything else—they must have thought that if they just found the right way to motivate me, eventually I would be able to drink without a straw. I'm sure that is the reason that Mom brought Kim Talbert into the picture. "How do you expect Kim to keep liking you if you never learn to drink without a straw?" she said, expecting her words to make a difference.

"I don't know," I replied.

"Maybe you better try again. Only this time, try a little harder."

After a couple of moments had gone by, Mom realized that her tactic wasn't working. "What do you think?" Mom asked, turning to Grandma Chance for moral support.

"I think that if Kim really cares for Steve, using a straw won't make any difference." Grandma confessed that she had wanted to stay out of it, but that once Mom asked for her opinion, she had to come to my defense.

Thanks, Grandma! I believed what she said then, and I believe it now. Unfortunately, the damage had already been done. I was being told that keeping Kim's friendship depended on my doing the impossible. I liked Kim, but there was no way, no matter how hard I tried, that I could lift that glass to my lips without making a mess. I was six years old, and from that day forward, I've seen my disability as something that prevents people, particularly girls, from liking me.

I don't blame Mom or harbor any bad feelings toward her for the remarks she made that day. She and Dad did an outstanding job of raising me, and I owe them both a great debt of gratitude for their efforts to give me the love and support that I needed in order to grow up and make something of my life. I love them both and would never want to hurt either of them. However, the idea that I can never measure up to other people's expectations because of something I can or cannot do is one that has stayed with me throughout my entire life for several reasons.

Contributing to my insecurities are the subtle messages that society sends to disabled persons. An unwritten law in America says that a person's worth is determined by his or her physical appearance and intellectual ability. If your body has the right shape to it and your mind has the right level of cognitive proficiency, then you are accepted as a valued member of society. But if your appearance is somehow blemished or your IQ is below what society says is acceptable, your worth as a person is questioned. The media constantly bombards each of us with messages of what it takes to be successful. It's only by having a perfect physique, the right hairstyle, and the latest in designer clothes that people can feel good about themselves. How can disabled people compete in a society that places so much emphasis on physical perfection? They can't. I can't. As a man with cerebral palsy, I live my life knowing that I will always fall short of the minimum standard set for acceptance by the mainstream of society.

I had been out of college for about five years and was seeking licensure as a pastor when I was confronted with the most blatant stereotyping imaginable. I drove down to the north side of Chicago to interview with a pastoral representative from the denomination. After asking me a few routine theological questions and some general questions about my philosophical approaches to ministry, he then proceeded to ask me questions that were much more personal in nature.

"Will you ever be able to satisfy a wife?" he continued, as if asking another routine question.

"I'm not sure what you mean," I lied.

"Will you be able to have sex?" he said, rephrasing the question.

I couldn't believe my ears. It was none of his business whether or not I could have sex. Besides, what does my ability to sustain an erection have to do with whether or not I would make a good pastor? Why would he ask such an intrusive question? My hunch is that he, at least on some level, equated manhood, possibly even personhood, with the ability to perform sexually. As ludicrous as this may sound, if you follow this line of thinking to its logical conclusion, it's no wonder that this minister of the gospel questioned my sexuality. After all, how can someone who doesn't measure up as a man fulfill his professional duties as a minister?

I wish I believed that this man is alone in his assumption that disabled people can't perform sexually and that they are therefore inferior to the rest of society. But I'm afraid that although most people might not be so blatant about their questions, deep down they share the same prejudice as that Chicago minister.

Even close friends have unknowingly contributed to my sense of not measuring up. I can't count the number of parties that I've attended during which someone has taken it upon himself to play the role of matchmaker. He starts by telling a woman at the party about a friend of his and then spends the next twenty minutes trying to figure out how to arrange for the two of them to meet.

I have always been a little envious of people who have friends to set them up on dates. Now, don't get me wrong. I'm not crying over spilt milk or launching a one-man crusade to start a dating service for people with disabilities. But I do think that we are often seen as less than ideal prospects for marriage partners. In many ways that perception is understandable. Everyone has fantasized about meeting Mr. or Miss Right, and usually those fantasies do not include someone with a disability.

It's important to note the impact of these messages, regardless of their subtlety, on disabled people. After a while, we begin to believe them. In my case, believing that I somehow fall short of society's expectations for normalcy has caused me immense feelings of shame over the years.

I feel a constant tension between two different aspects of my personality. The first is the fighter in me. I will fight tooth and nail to accomplish any goal that I set for myself and will defy anyone who tries to discourage me. No one stands in my way, and those who know me know that I will stand up to anything or anyone. Yet, another side of my personality isn't so strong. That side is the six-year-old boy who is desperately searching for a way to measure up but, despite how hard he tries, always feels hopelessly inadequate.

Nine

To Date or Not to Date

It is said that hindsight is always 20/20, and looking back on my life, I see many things that I wish I had done differently. Dating is one of them. I allowed my insecurities to get in the way of my common sense, and on many occasions simply blew what could have been very rewarding friendships.

I was a junior in high school when I had a big crush on a girl named Cindy Jackson. I had noticed her around campus and at the time thought that she was one of the best-looking girls I had ever seen. Never in my wildest dreams had I imagined that Cindy might be interested in me. Never, that is, until the day I went to the cafeteria early, only to have her come in about five minutes later.

"Can I sit here?" she asked, pulling out a chair on the other side of the table.

"Sure," I replied, not knowing what else to say.

Cindy sat down, and we were both so shy that neither of us said more than five words to each other during the entire meal.

To my surprise, Cindy came back again the next day. In fact, she came back every day for the next two months. Most guys would have caught on sooner or later to the fact that Cindy wasn't just looking for a place to eat her lunch. She liked me! She liked me, and I didn't have a clue! Instead of asking her out on a date, as I should have done, I did nothing. Every day it was the same story. We met in the cafeteria, found a table, ate lunch, and just looked at each other. Pathetic, isn't it? It's no wonder that Cindy found another lunch table after the semester break. It's not that she had stopped liking me. She had just given up on trying to get my attention—and who could blame her for that?

I blew it again during my senior year when I asked Pam McLaughlin to go to church with me one Sunday night. I can't remember what prompted me to ask her, except that she was pretty and kind of quiet. I was such a sucker for the quiet type back then. To my surprise, she accepted my invitation. For the next few months, we drove into Beloit once a week to attend the Sunday evening service at the First Church of the Open Bible. I liked Pam and did a little better with her than I had with Cindy. However, during all of the months that I took Pam to church, I never once asked her out on an actual date. That would have been too risky. If she had decided not to go to church with me, in my mind she would have been rejecting the church, not me. I had asked Pam out without the possibility of rejection. Looking back, I guess there's not much difference between asking a girl to church on a Sunday night and asking her to a movie and a pizza. I liked Pam, and she liked me. I was just too dense to see it.

I didn't see Pam again after I left for college. Taylor University was 300 miles away in Indiana, and I became too involved in other things to try to develop a long-distance relationship that wasn't going anywhere. We wrote back and forth to each other for a few months, and that was the end of it.

You may wonder why dating was so important to me. After all, the vast majority of teenagers didn't date when I was growing up. And of those who did, most dated very little. But for me, dating meant more than just going out with a girl on a Friday night or holding hands with her between classes. It was a sign of normalcy, a validation of who I was as a person. It was a goal that, when achieved, would mean that I was accepted as an equal in society.

By the same token, not dating, especially if it was somehow connected with my cerebral palsy, only reinforced the image I had of myself as being undatable. And in that area I did not need a lot of reinforcement. After all, who in her right mind would date someone with cerebral palsy when she could date any number of other guys who weren't disabled?

I was defeated before I even started. Everyone fears rejection when he first starts to date, but I was petrified. I was so scared of being turned down that I sabotaged my friendships. I made absolutely sure that I was never, ever rejected. It's not that I lacked friends. On the contrary, I had many friends—girlfriends, that is. Or, to be more accurate, I was friends with many, and I do mean many, girls. My problem was that I would never allow myself to go beyond the point of a platonic friendship with a girl whom I would much rather be dating. That's what I really wanted—to date. But trying to date would have allowed for the possibility of rejection, and that was something that, at that time, I felt I had to avoid at all cost.

My fears didn't vanish just because I went to college. I continued searching for acceptance and usually went about it in the wrong way. My first real date was with Sue Nelson, a pre-med student who was a year ahead of me in school. We went to a concert on campus during my first semester at Taylor, and I was once again hopelessly infatuated with the idea of falling in love. Sue's busy schedule didn't allow much time to socialize, but we did find time to eat some meals together and go for walks on campus. I had my trusty three-wheel bike with me, and from time to time Sue climbed into the rear basket and we'd go for a ride. We made quite a sight, Sue sitting in the basket and me pedaling my heart out.

I liked Sue. She was easy to talk with and a lot of fun to be around. We spent so much time together that the guys in the dorm began to wonder what was going on between the two of us. That was a good question, and I wasn't sure of the answer. That didn't matter to my floor mates, though. They made it clear that if there was any possibility of my wanting to date Sue, that I had to talk with her and let her know how I felt. And that's exactly what I did. I went over to her dorm and told her that I wanted to talk.

"What's up?" she asked, sensing my uneasiness.

"I want to ask you something, but I don't know how to start."

"I don't know what you're so nervous about. Just tell me what's on your mind."

"I like you, Sue. And, I think I want us to be more than just friends," I managed, fumbling for just the right words.

"I'm flattered, Steve," she said, becoming a little embarrassed. "I really do want to be good friends with you. But," she added, "I'm afraid that anything more than that is simply out of the question."

Good friends, huh? If that's not the story of my life, I don't know what is. I got turned down once and vowed to never let it happen again. There was just too much at stake. At the time, I didn't have the maturity to realize that someone might not want to go out with me for reasons other than discomfort with my cerebral palsy. I was stuck. Everything seemed connected to the cerebral palsy, but that was the one thing that I couldn't do anything about.

Things didn't change much during the next four years. I busied myself by spending time with guys in the dorms, occasionally looking at a book or two, and even going out on a few dates. Yet, in the midst of the hustle and bustle of college life, I was lost. I was doing everything possible to prove to myself—and to others— that I was just as capable as the next person of succeeding in the world. Yet in the one area that seemed to mean the most to me, dating, I felt utterly worthless. No matter what I did or how much I tried, I simply could never measure up to what I felt were other people's expectations of what it means to be a man. After all, I reasoned, how could I ever be accepted as potential dating material when I couldn't even hold a glass of water without spilling it all over the place?

Most people do not realize how much those of us with disabilities crave being in romantic relationships. Just because a person is in a wheelchair or has cerebral palsy does not mean that he or she lacks the desire for the same level of intimacy enjoyed by most of the rest of the world. Unfortunately, people see you differently if you're disabled. To most, the disabled person seems somehow asexual and is assumed to have either no desire or no capacity to enter into a meaningful relationship with someone of the opposite

sex. Let me tell you, that is simply not true. I am very much interested in romance, and so are most other disabled people I
know. However, the tension between wanting to be involved in a
relationship and getting lost in society's perceptions of disabled
persons can be excruciatingly painful.

Ten

Singing in the Rain

I first met Debbie Sheron in January 1980 during my senior year of college. She was a freshman and had just split up with a guy she had been dating during her first semester at Taylor. It was Friday night, and a group of us were looking for something to do. Someone suggested a movie, and before we knew it, a dozen of us had piled into the back of a pickup truck and headed for Muncie to see the movie *Kramer vs. Kramer*. I sat with my back to the cab next to Donna Pino, and Debbie sat on the other side of Donna. I rested my arm on the tool chest behind us and tried to stay warm. It can get cold in Indiana, especially when the temperature falls below zero at night, and we needed each other's body heat just to keep from freezing. There must have been ten of us in the back of the truck, and we were crammed in so tightly that none of us could move.

After the first five minutes of our half-hour drive into Muncie, Debbie's hand started hitting mine. "Go ahead and hold my hand until we get to the theater. After all," I added, with a touch of sarcasm, "that is what you have been trying to do ever since we left campus." I never expected Debbie to take my feeble attempt at humor seriously. She did, though, and without saying a word, Debbie slipped her hand into mine.

Sometimes guys can be a little dense, and I was one of the densest when it came to seeing the obvious. I should have asked Debbie out. Instead, we just started hanging around together. We did the usual—going to dinner, taking walks, and seeing an occasional movie—but never went on a real, serious, genuine, honest-to-goodness date. It didn't dawn on me until years later that if Debbie would hold my hand in the back of a pickup truck, chances are that she probably would have gone out with me. I should have asked her out, showed up at her dorm with flowers, treated her to the time of her life, and kissed her goodnight, promising to call the next day. That's what I should have done. Instead, I asked her out, took her to a movie, and when we got to the door of the theater, made her pay for her own ticket. Believe me, I know what you're thinking. And I've often regretted not doing things differently.

A few weeks later we saw another movie together—*Singing in the Rain*, with Gene Kelly, Donald O'Connell, and Debbie Reynolds. I forget who paid for the movie that night, not that it mattered. By that point, Debbie and I were such good friends that who paid was no longer an issue. What I do remember is showing up at her dorm, carrying an umbrella under my arm on a night when there wasn't a cloud in the sky.

"What is that?"

"It's an umbrella."

"I know that," Debbie said with a slight chuckle. "Why did you bring it?"

"I figure that if we are going to a musical about rain, the least I can do is play the part."

I think I had more fun that night than I had ever had in my life. Debbie and I walked down to the Pizza Inn afterward to get a bite to eat, and on the way I took out the umbrella, opened it up, and began dancing in the middle of the street. Debbie was having a pretty good time, too, and when I visited her more than a dozen years later, of all the things that we had done together, that's the night she remembered most. That night and the one when I took her to the movie and made her pay her own way. I'm not exactly proud of that episode, and I had hoped that after all these years Debbie might have forgotten about my ill-mannered behavior. Don't count on it! Although she is now married and lives in a different state, she still remembers.

I wasn't the only one around campus who had his eyes on Debbie that semester. Tom Wilson was a skinny freshman from Indiana who liked Debbie just as much as I did. She once told me about a date they had. When it was over, the poor guy looked at her and, with a straight face, asked if she minded being kissed because, he said, he had never kissed a girl before. I may have been pretty inept at dating, but even I knew that sounding desperate is the wrong way to impress a girl.

Sometimes Debbie and I would run into Tom around campus, and the look on his face when he saw the two of us together just tickled my insides all the way down to the bottom of my toes. I loved the idea of being the object of another guy's jealousy. That was a new experience for me, one that tended to be very good for my ego.

Now, I, of all people, know what it must have been like for Tom to see the two of us together. I've been in his shoes too many times to make light of his wanting something that he couldn't have. But I also have to admit that, for once in my life, it felt pretty good to know that someone else was left wanting what I had, instead of the other way around.

I really liked Debbie, and she and I became best friends that semester and spent at least some time together every day. Never in my life had I felt so close to someone. There was something about Debbie that made me feel good about myself as a person. She accepted me. She didn't care what other people thought and genuinely enjoyed spending as much time with me as possible. Yet, despite that acceptance, I never felt safe enough to be honest with her. For that matter, I never felt safe enough to be honest with myself, either. I could not admit to myself that I really liked Debbie and wanted her to be my girlfriend. I had plenty of friends. What I wanted was someone to date and eventually marry.

We went for a walk one Sunday in early spring and ended up down by the river, about a mile and a half from campus. It was one of those picturesque afternoons with the temperature just right and a slight breeze blowing through the trees. On the way home, I wanted more than anything to put my arm around her and tell her how much I cared for her. I almost did, too. I had my hand almost to her shoulders but pulled away at the last minute. I just couldn't do it.

It's one thing for two people not to date because that's what they both want. It's something else when one of them is haunted by so much shame that he finds it impossible even to broach the subject.

Debbie came to watch me graduate from Taylor at the end of May, and as I drove her home afterward I knew that I was saying goodbye to a big part of my life. I was going back to Wisconsin to work with Youth for Christ, and she had three more years left at Taylor. We wrote a lot that first summer, and when school started again she began dating Dave, the guy she had split up with eight months earlier. They married three years later, after finishing school, and I went to their wedding with Donna Pino, the gal who had sat between us in the pickup truck on the night we met. I even caught the garter, but that only added to my frustration. Debbie went home that night with Dave. I went home with a piece of blue cloth and memories of a friendship that could never be the same again.

I was excited for Debbie. She had found a good man that she dearly loved and will spend the rest of her life with. But at the same time I felt sorry for myself. I wanted the same kind of happiness that she and Dave had. For years I had been searching for that someone special to share my life with, and knowing Debbie Sheron was the closest I had ever come to finding her.

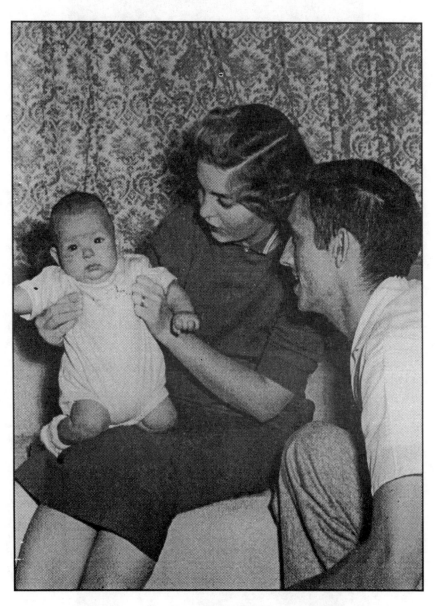

Steve at three months with Mom and Dad.

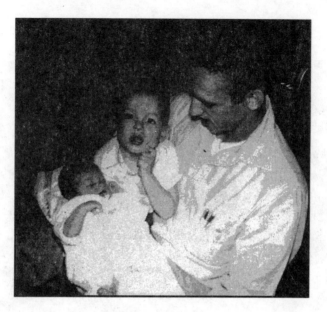

Steve, 2, between Bill and Dad.

Steve at two years, Bill at seven months.

Bill, 2, and Steve, 4, with Dr. Ellis
(who delivered Steve).

Bill, 6, and Steve, 8, Christmas 1966.

Steve on his first bike, age 7.

A boy and his dog, Blackie.

High school.

With college friend, Dave Brown, on graduation
day, Taylor University, 1980.

Steve's first camel ride, in Israel.

Covered with mud at the Dead Sea, during
Steve's college trip to Israel.

Bringing the house down with a stand-up comedy act at a college masquerade party.

Steve with Debbie Sheron during Taylor University's Youth Conference Weekend.

Mom and Dad with Susie.

Visiting college friends David and Debbie (Sheron) Entwistle
and daughters Lauren and Kristen, 1994.

Steve and brother, Bill, and Bill's bride, Amy.

Steve with his nieces and nephew –
Megan, Erica, Chas, and Jake.

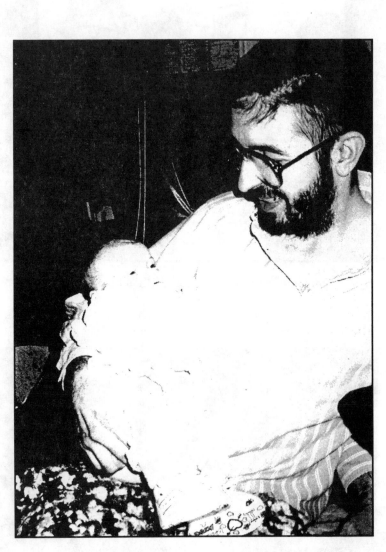

Holding seven-week-old niece Megan.

Wedding Day – May 21, 1988.

Mr. and Mrs. Steve Chance.

Groomsman Jeff Vander Wielen with Steve.

Enjoying married life.

Bob Pietsch, Kelly Sessions, and Steve reach the top
of a pyramid south of Mexico City during a
Golden Clay Ministries mission trip.

Rapelling down a 90-foot cliff in
California's High Sierra mountains.

Friend Del rappelling in a wheelchair.

Administrative Assistant Dottie Coleman
in Golden Clay Ministries' office.

Preaching in Hawaii.

Eleven

I'm Not Drunk—I Just Have Cerebral Palsy

I've heard it said that the number one phobia in America is the fear of speaking in front of a group of people. When I was a teenager, I was petrified at the thought of making class presentations or, worse yet, giving my testimony during church services. The sweaty palms were bad enough, but as the time approached for me to make my way to the front of the room, my entire body would start shaking from head to toe. I would have been off the scale if there was a Richter measurement for people with cerebral palsy. And what they tell you about picturing your audience in their underwear? It doesn't work.

That's why it was so out of character for me to agree to do a stand-up comedy routine at a costume party during my junior year at Taylor. I came as the town drunk. Now, in no way do I condone alcoholism or want to give the impression that there's anything humorous about public intoxication. But having said that, let me assure you of one thing. When I walked out on stage that night, I was outrageously funny.

Two men, both bombed out of their minds, were walking along some railroad tracks. The first guy complained that the "steps" were too low—they had been "climbing" for more than an hour, and neither had yet reached the second floor. The second guy had

his own problems and spent the entire afternoon trying to figure
out why the "handrails" were so close to the ground.

That joke may not be funny in print. But when a guy with
cerebral palsy, sporting a trench coat, a lady's wig, and a wine
bottle partially hidden in a paper sack, gets up on stage and tells
it, it's hilarious. Two hundred people were at that party, and
some of them were laughing so hard they were crying. That was a
good night for me. I received more accolades than I ever had before, and all because of a couple of bad jokes and an audience willing to laugh at anything.

Of course, that wasn't the only time in my life that I've appeared to have had a little too much to drink. If you have cerebral
palsy, looking tipsy comes with the territory, and I've had my so-
briety questioned on more than one occasion. I was coming home
from a high school football game one night when some kid started
yelling at me from across the field.

"Hey! You over there! Did you have a little too much fun at
the ball game?"

He saw the way I was walking, was convinced that I was
plastered, and was out to tell the world about it. I wasn't
drunk—not even close. The only thing I had that night was cerebral palsy, and I certainly was guilty of having too much of that.

I was mad, and I wanted in the worst way to tell this guy
that there's a difference between having a disability and getting
tipsy at a ball game. But what good would it have done? He
didn't care one iota about whether I was drunk or, for that matter, if I was visiting from Mars. He just needed someone to pick
on, and I was an easy target.

I was in Beloit a few years later and stopped at a friend's
place one afternoon to see if anyone was home. I entered the front
of the building, located his apartment, and knocked on the door.
When no one answered, I left. About three minutes later, I was
driving down the road when two squad cars pulled behind me.

"Can I see your driver's license?" one of the officers asked after
pulling me over.

"What seems to be the problem?" I asked, rummaging
through my billfold.

"Were you just at one of the apartment buildings up the street?"

"Only for a minute. I went to see a friend. He wasn't home, so I left. Why?"

"A neighbor called to report a break-in by someone appearing to be intoxicated."

"What?" I exclaimed, not believing what I had just heard.

Cerebral palsy? Yes! Intoxicated? I don't think so! That reminds me of the man with cerebral palsy who was pulled over by the police on three different occasions for being "under the influence"—once while driving and twice while walking. If the police hadn't seen that I was disabled, I would have spent the day in jail, trying to sleep off cerebral palsy.

Sure, I can joke about it now. But you try going through life never knowing when someone is going to crack a joke at your expense or give you a funny stare from across the room. The worst part is that I never know when an incident is going to occur. I could be at the post office, at a grocery store, or just walking down the street, minding my own business. It can happen anywhere and at any time. I've been called all sorts of names by people who don't even know me, patted on the back by patronizing salesmen who think they're doing me a favor, and simply ignored by store clerks who find it easier to pretend that I don't exist than to acknowledge my presence.

I'm sure that you have seen all the stereotypical scenes that are shown on television, showing how the public treats disabled persons. They're true. Such incidents really do happen. I've lost count of the number of times that waitresses have asked other people in my group what I want to eat instead of asking me directly. Once I even had a church secretary call and ask to speak to my "dad." I told her that Dad lives 2000 miles away and reminded her that she had called me. I was only returning her call, I said, and when she figured out what she wanted to say, she could call back. She realized her mistake, apologized, and then proceeded to invite me to speak at her church for a Disability Awareness Sunday. She worked with disabled people; she of all people, therefore, should have known better.

I hate phones! Operators call me ma'am, business people ask for my parents, and one guy even offered to call an ambulance for me. I would have let him, too, if I had thought it would help. I wasn't sick—I just wasn't talking as clearly as he expected.

Something similar happened a few years later when a salesman called to tell me about the 40% savings I would gain if I switched to his particular long-distance service. I politely interrupted him, said I wasn't interested in changing phone companies, and hung up the receiver. A couple of moments later, the phone rang again. It was the same man, calling back to tell me how "constipated" I sounded when I spoke. Can you believe it? Maybe I do sound a little constipated when I speak, but that doesn't mean I want to be told about it by some disgruntled salesman trying to blow off steam because he failed to make a sale.

I could probably write a whole book on how disabled people are treated in public. Every time someone makes a rude comment or does something blatantly inappropriate, I want to cry out in anger. How dare people treat me with so little respect that they won't even acknowledge my presence? I don't have a lot of patience with people who purposely ignore someone just because of the way he looks or talks. It's rude, it's uncalled for, and I would just as soon not have to deal with it. It would be nice to wake up one morning and know that for that day—for the entire day—I could go anywhere I wanted to go and do anything I wanted to do and not wonder whether someone would make an issue of my cerebral palsy. But that will never happen, at least not in this lifetime. Regardless of how much I might wish that things were different, I know that there will always be people who are unwilling to accept me as an equal member of society.

I am not talking about the person who for some reason or another doesn't know what to say or how to act around me because of my disability. Many people are afraid of doing or saying the wrong thing and, instead of taking the chance of being offensive, take the easy way out and choose not to do or say anything. I understand where they're coming from, and I can accept that. What I cannot accept is the arrogance of some people who go out of their way to be rude. That's intolerable, and I hate it. I deserve better than that. I deserve to be treated with the same level of dignity and respect that anyone else would receive. I more than deserve it—I demand it! And if anyone fails to give me that respect, he or she had better watch out, because I have no difficulty in asserting myself. I don't hesitate to let people know when they've crossed the line—if not verbally, then I find some other way to let them know that their actions are inappropriate. You'd be surprised at what holding eye contact does to a guy who's been staring at me for the past five minutes from the other side of the room. It catches him off guard. He doesn't know whether to turn away or to keep staring, and for that one tiny moment, that person is the one who is feeling uncomfortable. If he turns away, that act is an admission of guilt, and if he continues to look, then I continue the eye contact.

Now, I don't want to get into a debate over whether my way of combating rudeness is the best solution to the problem. I'm sure that if you posed the question to a hundred different people, some would say that it is and others would say that it isn't. That's not the point. The point is that it happens, and when it does happen, I do something about it. And if some people become educated about what is and what is not acceptable in the process, so much the better.

Can you believe what I just said? I may sound tough, but the truth is that whenever I am confronted by someone who makes an issue of my disability, a part of me just wants to crawl into a hole and hide. I grow tired of constantly being on my guard, of never knowing when and where my presence will make someone else uncomfortable. I hate knowing that whenever I walk down the street, I might meet someone who would just as soon cross to the other side of the road than have to walk past me.

You may be reading this and thinking to yourself that it's not my problem if other people don't know how to act around disabled persons, it's their problem. I wish that were true, but it doesn't work that way. It is my problem. Oh, sure, I can ignore people and pretend that they don't exist. I can even pretend that the things they say don't hurt. But that wouldn't be true. I may have a few more emotional calluses now than I did when I was a kid, but even now that I am an adult, some of the things that people say do hurt. I was told as a kid that "sticks and stones may break my bones, but words will never hurt me." Guess what? Words do hurt, and they hurt a lot.

Every time someone makes a rude comment or acts in a way that he or she wouldn't have if I weren't disabled, I'm reminded that I'm just a little bit different from almost everyone else. And because of that difference, I face an unending battle of having to prove myself. At least, that's the way I see it. I have to prove that I am just as capable of living a meaningful and productive life with cerebral palsy as I would be without cerebral palsy. Now, I know I don't really have to prove anything to anyone but myself, that it's only what I believe that's important. Maybe the real problem is that I've been told so many times and in so many ways that I don't measure up, that somewhere along the line I've actually begun to believe it.

Twelve

Going Home

Youth for Christ had made such a lasting impact on my life that, after finishing college, I returned to Beloit to work full-time with Dick Myers. I wanted to reach high school kids for Christ in the same way that I had been reached years earlier, and as a staff person I had the opportunity to do just that. I worked for Stateline Youth for Christ for four years and, during that time, discovered that I loved working in ministry. I was pretty good at it, too.

At the time, Stateline had club ministries in Beloit, Clinton, and Orfordville. I was in charge of the Beloit and Orfordville clubs, and at one point, I was running what was then the second-largest program in the state of Wisconsin. I don't take a lot of credit for that achievement. I was just fortunate enough to recruit some exceptional volunteer staff members during the first few months there, and they're the ones who deserve the real credit for whatever success we may have had.

I worked with a lot of good volunteers during my years at Youth for Christ, but one in particular, Jeff Vander Wielen, comes to mind. Jeff wasn't your typical Youth for Christ volunteer. He had been more interested in getting high on marijuana during high school than in going to class, and it showed. His grades were lousy, and he managed to graduate only by the skin of his teeth. It took a few years, but Jeff finally turned his life around. He became a Christian, worked at a couple of jobs in Texas, and moved to Beloit in the summer of 1980. That's when I talked him into volunteering with the Beloit YFC club, and for the next three years Jeff and I worked together in ministry.

I liked Jeff. He was down to earth and easy to talk with, and the kids loved him. It didn't take very long for the two of us to become the best of friends, and before I knew it we were spending three or four evenings a week together. We were the perfect team, and his popularity certainly made my job easier. All I had to worry about were logistics: planning club meetings, putting together special events, and getting everything ready for camp. Jeff, on the other hand, spent a lot of his free time with kids. We loved to camp, and YFC's winter camp was the best. The same camp that I had gone to as a teenager, I now attended as a staff member, and Jeff was always there to help. Some years, we took as many as 70 teenagers into northern Wisconsin for three fun-filled, action-packed days of playing in the snow.

Tradition had it that a talent show was held every year, and one time Jeff and I decided to give the show a new twist. We conducted an in-depth comparative study between the guys' restroom and the gals' restroom, both of which were located in the basement of the main lodge. Since none of the cabins were equipped with plumbing (which probably explains the yellow snow that appeared periodically outside the boys' cabins throughout the night) these restrooms were the only two restrooms in camp.

We talked one of the female staff members into escorting us into the gals' restroom and were absolutely dumbfounded by what we saw. Compared to the guys' restroom, it was the Taj Mahal of camping, complete with curtains, flowers, wallpaper, and even individual shower stalls. We, on the other hand, were forced to make do with a shower room built out of cinder blocks, with four or five faucets sticking out of the wall. There were no flowers, no curtains, and a lousy paint job; it didn't even come close to the room that we had seen on the other side of the building.

Now, I personally didn't mind the disparity between the two rooms. But when Jeff and I got up later that evening to report our findings, you would have thought that a bomb had just exploded in the main lodge. The gals were stunned, the guys were outraged, and the camp staff were really embarrassed—so much so that when we returned the following year, major improvements had been made in the guys' shower room.

I had so much fun on those camping trips, even when I was the butt of a practical joke. One night, Jeff and I were in the restroom together. I was at the sink, and Jeff was in one of the stalls. Before coming out, he had removed the lid from the toilet tank and scraped out a handful of sludge.

"I ran out of toilet paper," Jeff said, showing me the contents of his hand.

I almost lost it.

"Steve, it's a joke," he yelled, trying to catch me as I ran out of the restroom.

"Some joke," I said, managing not to get sick. He hadn't counted on the fact that I had a weak stomach.

That brings me to my next story. One summer, Jeff and I took a road trip down to Corpus Christi, Texas. While there, we decided to try our hand at some deep-sea fishing off the Gulf of Mexico. We arrived at the harbor around 6:30 A.M. to catch the boat that would take us on our eight-hour fishing expedition. I made three mistakes that morning. The first was not eating before leaving the house. I couldn't quite stomach the cow's tongue that everyone was having, so I decided to forego breakfast. I made my second mistake about half an hour after we left port, when I decided to walk to the front of the boat. The water was choppy, and I wanted to see how it felt to be up front as the boat hit the waves. That was not a good idea. With each wave, the boat rose twenty feet into the air before coming down with a crash. Up and down, up and down, over and over again. The temperature was near a hundred, there wasn't a cloud in the sky, and I had an empty stomach—a lethal combination, to be sure.

It didn't take long to feel the effects of my stupidity. I was sick, and there wasn't a thing I could do about it. I tried sitting down, walking around, and even lying down on a bench in the rear of the boat, but it was too late. I was getting sicker and sicker by the minute and figured it was about time for me to make my way over to the side of the boat. That was my third mistake. How was I to know that the best place to be when getting sick in a boat is in the rear? Throwing up over the side of a boat has the same effect as spitting in the wind. Need I say more? Let's just say that for me it wasn't a fun trip.

As sick as I was, though, whenever the boat stopped and it was time to fish, I always had my line in the water. I may have been puking my guts out, but I had paid $40 for that trip and wasn't about to let anything rob me of the chance to catch the "big one." It would have helped if I had been able to catch something that day, but no such luck. I had one bite, but that was it. Jeff didn't fare any better. Dwayne, the other guy in our group, came home with two sharks, so I guess the day wasn't a complete waste. Still, I wish that at least one of those sharks had been mine. All I had was a severe sunburn and some vomit stuck to my tennis shoe. Those aren't the kind of souvenirs that you want to bring home from a vacation.

Jeff and I did a lot of fishing, and during the summer months we were out on the lake at least twice a week. We both had our own canoes, and we made it a practice to meet after work and fish until dark. We loved to fish. It didn't matter how much it rained or how low the temperature dropped; if the fish were biting, we were on the lake with our lines in the water. Jeff was in back, I was in front, and between the two of us we fished with four poles.

Strange things happen to people when they spend so much time in the sun. They become selfish, especially when one guy is catching fish and the other guy needs to go ashore. "I think we'd better leave," one of us would exclaim, usually after putting off going to the bathroom for as long as possible.

"But I just had a bite," the other would respond, knowing that both of us had to be willing to pull up our anchors in order to go ashore.

After a minute or so, the person who wanted to keep fishing generally gave in without much of an argument. It was dangerous to wait too long before agreeing to go ashore, because we both knew that the next time out the shoe might be on the other foot.

Between the two of us, we caught a lot of fish. Sometimes we had to go home empty-handed, and on those days, we drove to a restaurant and ordered ourselves a fish dinner. There's nothing worse for a fisherman than admitting failure, but by going out to eat, we could truthfully say that we had gotten our share of fish. They might have been caught by someone else, cooked, and brought to us on a plate with lots of French fries and coleslaw on the side, but that was all we needed to boast of a successful fishing trip.

Jeff and I loved to eat almost as much as we loved to fish. One night, shortly after Jeff began working in the Beloit club, we met early and went to the Pizza Inn just down the road from the office. The two of us split a large, deep-dish pan pizza with everything on it. It was without a doubt the best pizza I ever had, but we paid for it afterward. Jeff and I had stuffed ourselves, and neither of us felt much like leading a club meeting. We had no choice, though. The kids were showing up around seven, and we were the ones in charge. We were too embarrassed to tell the kids that we weren't feeling well, so we took turns up front, looking like we were about to keel over. Somehow we made it through the night and then vowed never to eat that much pizza again.

Jeff lived in Beloit for three years, and during that time we became closer than brothers. His experience in working with club kids spurred him on to higher goals. In the fall of 1983, Jeff left Beloit to attend the University of Wisconsin at Steven's Point as a psychology major. I felt as though I was losing a part of myself when he left Beloit. I do not make close friends easily. Jeff was the closest friend I've ever had. He stayed at Steven's Point for a year before transferring to Westmont College, in Santa Barbara, California. That's when we began losing touch with each other. He lived in California and then moved to Idaho. I lived in Wisconsin and then moved to Illinois and later to New York. We simply went our separate ways. We still keep in touch and occasionally see each other. We were even in each other's weddings. But that's not the same as the ongoing camaraderie that we shared as two single men living in Wisconsin, spending our evenings trying to outdo each other with fishing poles while sitting in a boat out on a lake.

In all of the years that I worked with Youth for Christ, my cerebral palsy became an issue only once. Jeff and I were out one night with a couple of club kids, Paul Lee and Larry Smith, when Larry began telling us about an uneasiness that some of the kids in the Beloit club felt.

"What do you mean, they feel uneasy?" I asked.

"Some of the kids just happened to mention that something about the club makes them comfortable."

"Well, did they say what it is?"

"Yeah, but I don't think I should tell you."

"Why not?"

"I just shouldn't," Larry said, without any further elaboration.

I'm usually not one to be intrusive, but this was different. I was in charge of the Beloit club. And if there was something going on to make some of the kids uncomfortable, I wanted to know about it. It was one thing not to say anything about the situation. It was something else entirely for Larry to tell me that something was going on and then refuse to tell me what that something was. Every time I asked for an explanation, he refused to give one. His excuse? It wasn't his responsibility to tell me what the other kids were thinking. Poppycock! If it wasn't his responsibility, then he shouldn't have said anything in the first place. But once he did, how could he then refuse to give us any further explanation? He couldn't. At least, that's how I saw it.

Jeff agreed with me, and so did Paul, and the three of us spent a full hour trying to convince Larry to tell us what was going on. Finally he admitted that my cerebral palsy was bothering a few of the kids. Imagine that! My disability prevented a couple of teenagers from coming to some of our activities. I knew that.

I realized early on in my ministry that my cerebral palsy might prevent some people from giving me a chance, and I could drive myself batty by worrying about all those who might be turned off by my disability. I decided not to do that. No one person can be all things to all people, and even if I weren't disabled, some people would remain unresponsive to my ministry. I know that, and I accept that. Yet I also know that for every person who allows my disability to be an obstacle to his coming to a meeting, there stands another person who welcomes my ministry abilities with open arms. And I believe that those are the people to whom God has called me to minister his gospel.

The fact is, despite Larry's perception of how the other teens felt, I had a very good rapport with most of the people who came to our clubs. So much so that I would probably still be at Youth for Christ today if it weren't for the friction that arose between myself and the executive director. I could write volumes about what went wrong or who's to blame for my leaving Youth for Christ. But that is not the intent of this book, and pointing fingers would serve no useful purpose. Suffice it to say that I left Stateline Youth for Christ in August of 1984, and that I did not do so under the best of circumstances.

As difficult as things had become at YFC, deciding to leave was one of the hardest decisions that I've ever made in my life. Although it's true that I loved youth ministry, my true dilemma was that I was terrified of leaving. I was just too afraid of looking for work elsewhere, and I felt trapped. Youth for Christ was safe. I was known in Beloit and had already proven myself as someone capable of performing quality work. I was afraid that no other employer would give me the same chance to prove myself that Youth for Christ had given me.

My fear of permanent unemployment kept me at YFC a full six months longer than I should have stayed. As a matter of fact, it was my fear that had brought me to Youth for Christ in the first place. I had always wanted to work at Stateline YFC, but in some ways I took the easy way out by returning to Wisconsin after graduating from college. I never even considered looking elsewhere for work. I was too afraid to try. I could not risk being told that I wasn't suitable for a job, knowing full well that the reason behind that decision was my cerebral palsy. That would have been unbearable. I'm glad that I went to work with YFC, but I wish that I had done so for the right reasons and not out of a fear that no other options existed for me.

A part of any job search is being told by employers that you're not exactly the type of person they're looking for. I know that. Everyone faces the prospect of having the door slammed in his or her face while looking for work. I also know that most people, if given enough time, will eventually find work. Although I believed that to be true for other people, I didn't believe that it was true for me. Instead of having confidence in my ability to find work, I was convinced that no one would ever hire me, regardless of how many applications I submitted or how many interviews I had.

I was sure that I could easily find work, if only I could figure out a way to present myself to potential employers so that my cerebral palsy wouldn't show. That was asking for the impossible, though. Everywhere I go, this disability called cerebral palsy goes with me, and there isn't a thing I can do about it. Cerebral palsy isn't something that I can take off right before a job interview and put on again once I've landed a position. It's with me every single day of my life, and no matter how much I try to hide it, it is always out there for everyone to see.

Thirteen

Heartache

I was out of college for three years when I started dating my first real girlfriend. A group of us went to a ball game one night and then to Sandy Nolan's apartment afterward for some cookies and punch.

"Can you stay a little longer?" Sandy asked, after the last group of stragglers began to leave.

"Sure," I said, not thinking anything of the invitation.

The two of us chatted for another fifteen minutes, and I got up to leave for a second time. As I was saying good night, she reached up and asked me for a hug. That's when Sandy told me that she liked me and asked if we could date.

I went home that night on top of the world. After twenty-five years, I had finally found someone who wanted to love and accept me just for me. All my fears of being undatable were swept away with one hug, a kiss, and the promise of a tomorrow with plenty of emotional intimacy, something I had craved for years.

A week went by before I began telling people that Sandy and I were dating. It took that long for me to believe it myself. Boy, were our friends surprised. Never in their wildest dreams had any of them imagined the two of us together. Sandy was a couple of years older than I, and we had first met in high school. She had taken a few years off after graduating before coming to Taylor University in the middle of my junior year. I had enjoyed having someone there from my hometown, and it had been natural for us to start spending time together. To make a long story short, we started out at Taylor as friends, but it didn't take long for that friendship to sour. She had her eyes on Lyle Davis, a friend of mine from Hill House. Once she had easy access to Lyle, she let me know in no uncertain terms that I was no longer needed. She tried blowing me off while at the same time wanting to maintain the appearance of a friendship. She wanted to use me to continue putting the moves on Lyle, and when she learned that I wasn't going to play ball, things became pretty cold between the two of us.

None of that mattered in the summer of 1983. We had both moved back to Wisconsin, had patched up our differences, and now were dating. Life was good, or so I thought.

Little did I know that the euphoria I had felt during the first few weeks of our relationship would not last. Before long, the "honeymoon" stage was over, and by the second month, we were fighting about everything from how much time to spend together to whether or not we would have a dog if and when we decided to marry. I kid you not. Sandy was so adamant against having a pet that she wanted me to vow never, ever to buy a dog, regardless of any frantic begging our future kids might do. That's right. It didn't take us very long to bring up the "m" word—her idea, not mine. I'm ashamed of even considering marrying someone who was so obviously wrong for me. Yet the prospect of marriage, even to Sandy, was important to me, and we talked openly about our hopes of one day settling down together. As I recall, those discussions didn't last for more than a couple of weeks—the time it took her to decide she didn't really want to marry me. However, it took us much longer than that to stop dating.

Sandy was in love with the idea of being in love. She had an image of what she wanted in life, and it included a husband, four or five kids, and a house in the country with a white picket fence around the front yard. She knew exactly what she was looking for, and it didn't include a man with cerebral palsy. Her dream man had long blondish hair and a beard and wore a green flannel shirt. Just imagine a lumberjack, and you'll have a pretty good idea of the kind of man Sandy was looking for.

I hope you don't think I'm making all of this up. I'm not. Sandy herself told me.

"Look! Look! There he is!" she shouted one evening while we were sitting on the couch.

"Who?"

"That's the guy I want to marry!" she said, holding up a magazine and pointing to a picture of a guy much like the one I just described.

If that wasn't enough, she then took a pair of scissors, clipped out the picture, and taped it to the refrigerator door. I knew then that I could never measure up to Sandy's expectations of what she wanted in a man, but that didn't stop me from trying. Oh, how I tried. I did everything that I could think of to make our relationship work, and the harder I tried, the more we fought.

So why didn't I just break up with Sandy if things were so bad between us? I could have saved myself a lot of heartache if I had ended the relationship after the first few months, as I should have. Yet I didn't. I couldn't. For years, I had searched for someone to love and accept me just as I was. I was sure that breaking up with Sandy meant giving up all my dreams for the future. It was just too hard to admit that the fears and insecurities I had so long felt about being undatable might have been true. I continued dating Sandy a full year longer than I should have simply because my fears of being alone made breaking up unthinkable.

Deep down, I knew that my disability would always prevent Sandy and me from having a life together. I kept wishing for the impossible, that she would somehow be able to look past the cerebral palsy to the real me inside. She couldn't—but still I hoped. I hoped for the one chance in a million to convince her that I was indeed lovable, despite the cerebral palsy.

Looking back, I believe that Sandy did try to make things work. She tried to love me. She just went about it in the wrong way. She thought that she could love me without loving the disability. She tried loving me and ignoring my disability. She tried loving me and tolerating my disability. Then she tried loving me and rejecting my disability. When that didn't work, she tried faking it, but that didn't work either. By rejecting my cerebral palsy, she also rejected me. It did no good for Sandy to say that she loved me and at the same time say that she wished I were different. Sandy didn't love me. She loved the guy she wanted me to be.

My dream world was shattered one Sunday after church. We were walking along the side of the road, holding hands and looking at the fields in the distance, when out of nowhere came a quizzical look in her eyes. She took one step backward, looked at me, and asked, "Steve, is there any way, if you try really hard, that you could walk a little straighter?"

I was mad! It had taken me twenty-six years of effort to walk as well as I walked that day, and still that wasn't good enough for Sandy. How dare she!

I should have ended the relationship then and there. But even then my hopes for marriage prevented me from breaking up with Sandy. That didn't come until a couple of months later, when I finally decided that spending the rest of my life by myself was preferable to life with Sandy. Nevertheless, letting go of my relationship with her was one of the hardest things that I've done in my life. I was convinced that by saying goodbye to Sandy I was condemning myself to a life of loneliness. It had taken me twenty-five years to find Sandy, and now all my hopes were gone. I feared loneliness, but I knew by then that being alone, even for the rest of my life, was better than another week of being with Sandy.

Fourteen

Thomson, Without the "P"

After leaving Stateline Youth for Christ, I had been out of work for six months when I received a pastoral call from a Congregational church in Thomson, Illinois. I was ecstatic at the thought of having my own church and arrived in Thomson in February 1985 with all kinds of energy and enthusiasm.

Thomson is a tiny farm town of 550 people and sits on the east bank of the Mississippi River, about 50 miles directly west of Rockford, Illinois. When I first read the name "Thomson" in print, I thought there had been a typographical error. I assumed, wrongly, that I was moving to Thompson, spelled with a "p." But there is no town of Thompson in Illinois, and as far as I know there never has been. In fact, the standing joke in town is that the only "p" in Thomson is during the watermelon season. That's my kind of humor!

Thomson Community Church was one of three churches in town and had a congregation of around 40 members. The people expected a well-developed sermon on Sunday mornings; a monthly visit to each of their homes; weekly nursing home visits; and someone to officiate at weddings, funerals, and baptisms. That was it, and for my first six months in town I loved pastoring the church.

In a town as small as Thomson, there wasn't much for a single man to do with his spare time. There were only so many times in one week that I could visit people without wearing out my welcome, and after fulfilling my duties as a pastor, I still had time left over. That's when I went out to the Durwood's.

Cliff Durwood and his three sons operated a dairy farm a few miles outside of Thomson, and all four of them welcomed me with open arms. They knew a good deal when they saw it, and on my first visit they put a shovel in my hand and told me to go to work cleaning out the barn. They milked close to fifty head of cattle twice a day—once in the morning and then again at night. That many animals in one building can produce an unbelievable amount of manure, and it all had to be shoveled out every day.

The thing that I appreciated most about the Durwoods was that they didn't care whether or not I was the pastor of a local church, someone from out of town, or a guest from another country. To them I was just Steve Chance, a man willing to help out in any way he could. Cliff and his sons treated me the same way that they treated everyone else who came out to the farm. If they felt like cussing, they cussed. If they felt like lighting up a cigar, they lit up a cigar. And if they felt like having a beer, they did that too. They did anything they felt like doing, and they weren't about to let some up-and-coming preacher keep them from having their fun.

Now, you might think that all of the Durwoods' crude language and barnyard behavior might have turned me off, but it had just the opposite effect. Being a minister can sometimes become pretty suffocating, and everywhere I went people were always on their best behavior, afraid to let me see them for who they really were. I found it immensely refreshing to be around people who felt free enough to be themselves and not have to hide behind a facade of Christianized jargon every time I came around.

I spent a lot of time at the Durwood farm, and I usually came home feeling exhausted from working too hard, yet exhilarated from pushing myself to the limit. Some days I helped with the feeding, and on other days I cleaned out the barns. In the spring and summer I helped with the haying, and in the fall I helped with the corn harvest. And when I became really desperate for something to do, I drove the five miles to the Durwood's other farm and spent the day chasing pigs onto an old horse trailer used to transport animals to market. That was not a fun job. Cleaning out a dairy barn is one thing, but there's nothing like the smell of hôgs on a really warm day. It's awful. In fact, it's bad enough to turn a diehard meat-and-potatoes man into a vegetarian on the spot. But somebody had to do the job, and I wasn't about to wimp out just because of an odor that was a little too pungent.

You wouldn't believe how much manure can accumulate when fifteen or twenty litters of pigs are all crammed under one roof. When it came time to clean, every bit of straw, manure, and urine had to be removed and the floor swept. To make the job easier, someone had turned a 55-gallon drum into a dump-cart that ran along a track mounted to the ceiling. Instead of having to go back and forth all the time with a wheelbarrow, we filled the cart up at the far end of the building and pushed the manure down the track and out the door.

It's amazing what a little old-fashioned ingenuity can do, and the dump-cart idea saved us a lot of time and effort. Of course, there was that one time when someone forgot to replace the piece of track that went underneath the door frame. Without it, the cart couldn't be pushed outside. It was a disaster just waiting to happen, and Cliff was the unfortunate one pushing the dump-cart when it jumped off the track. Before he could react, he was standing knee deep in a ton of pig doo-doo. Cliff was mad, and he let everyone know it.

"Who's the boneheaded idiot that left that track gate undone?" he shouted, adding a few expletives out of anger.

I may not have been the one who forgot to fasten the track gate, but I knew enough to keep my mouth shut until Cliff cooled off. I guess I wouldn't have been very happy either if 80 pounds of manure had just fallen on top of me. There have been times in my life that I have felt like I've been in the basement of an outhouse, looking up with my mouth opened, but only because I've had a bad day. In this case, it really happened, though, and Cliff made sure that we knew to never let it happen again.

I know that some people reading this are scratching their heads and wondering why in the world anyone would willingly volunteer to clean out a hog barn. That's a good question, and looking back, I sometimes wonder about it myself. Why did I ever hook up with a bunch of guys who spent their days making hay, milking cows, and shoveling manure? After all, most people don't spend their leisure time this way. The truth is that although I enjoyed physically exerting myself, I was mostly looking for a place to plug into in a community where I otherwise felt isolated.

The Durwoods gave me a place to belong. They invited me not only out to their farm but into their lives as well. One night they even took me to the dog races over in Iowa for an experience I'll never forget. Three of us drove an hour and a half one way, just to watch greyhounds chase after a stuffed rabbit.

When I first moved to Thomson, I fully intended to make it my home for quite a few years. I even purchased a house a few months after moving there, which turned out to be one of the biggest mistakes of my life. It was too much house. I really didn't need a three-bedroom, two-story home to take care of, and I don't know what possessed me to buy such a huge house in the first place. It took an incredible amount of time to care for, not to mention the financial drain on my savings account.

The money wasn't the worst part. Owning a home locked me into the community. That was okay as long as I wanted to stay in Thomson, but the moment I decided that the time had come to move on, the house became a ball and chain tying me to the area. It didn't take long for that to happen, and as soon as six months later I talked to someone about putting the house back on the market.

"The only people who move into Thomson are pastors and schoolteachers," the realtor told me in the beginning of December. "The earliest I expect anyone to look at your house will be sometime in early spring."

That wasn't exactly what I had wanted to hear. "We can't lose anything by trying," I said, hoping for what seemed to be the impossible.

I decided to put the house on the market, despite the realtor's pessimism, and I'm glad I did. Before a month had gone by, someone expressed an interest in looking at it. I had six-hours' notice before showing the house and spent the entire afternoon cleaning. I was more than ready to get out of Thomson, but in order to do that, I needed to sell the house. I did everything I could think of in order to make the house as attractive as possible to the potential buyer.   From scrubbing floors to washing windows, I cleaned every room.   The effort paid off, and before the week was out I had accepted an offer to buy the house.

So what was it like for me, a man with cerebral palsy, to be the spiritual leader of a church?   It was horrible! I made a lousy pastor, and I'm afraid the reasons that I made a lousy pastor had little to do with my disability. Thomson was a wonderful town to live in, and the people in the congregation were very kind and gracious to me during my employment at the church. Yet despite all the warmth and hospitality shown me, when it came right down to it, I just wasn't cut out to be a pastor. In fact, of all the things that I have done in ministry, pastoring the Thomson Community Church is probably the one thing at which I considered myself a failure.

Although it's true that I felt lonely and isolated, the real reason behind my leaving the church is that I felt that I had failed as a pastor. I failed the people who had hired me by not providing the spiritual guidance and direction they deserved; I failed myself by not doing the kind of job that I knew I could have done. And, ultimately, I felt I had failed God by not being the type of minister that I thought he had called me to be.

Cognitively, I am very much aware of how my ministry in Thomson impacted some of the parishioners of the church. However, there's a part of me that knows I did not measure up to my fullest potential as a minister. Sure, I preached every Sunday. I baptized people. I even officiated at weddings and funerals. I was very good at being with people and performing all the ceremonial functions that went along with being a pastor. But when it came to nurturing people's faith, I was ill prepared to minister full-time in a church. I was only in my mid-twenties and knew nothing about ministering with adults. All of my training had been in youth work; I lacked direction, for myself and for the church, and I was too ashamed to ask anyone for help. So I did the only thing I knew to do. I left.

I knew what I *didn't* want for my life—I didn't want to stay in Thomson, and I didn't want to be a pastor. Yet I had no idea what I *did* want. So as soon as escrow closed on the house, I headed down to Taylor University. I still had a lot of friends there and wanted their input about what I should do next. I talked to anybody and everybody, including Lowell Haines, the dean of students at Taylor. Lowell had been the hall director at Sammy Morris Hall for two of the three years that I had lived there, and I believed that if anyone could give me advice on what to do, he could.

"Houghton College has a cooperative program in student development with Buffalo State College," Lowell offered. "Maybe if you write the dean of students, there still might be time to get into the program."

I took Lowell's advice. When I heard back from Houghton a short time later, I had only one week to respond before the final deadline for applying for the fall enrollment. I worked my butt off that week! I spent the time filling out applications (both for Houghton and for Buffalo), gathering recommendations, and writing essays about myself and why I desired to pursue a career in student development. I wrote, rewrote, and then rewrote each essay again until I had it worded just the way I wanted it. I wanted the applications to be as perfect as possible before I dropped them into the mail. I was really looking forward to getting out of Thomson, and I didn't want to do anything to jeopardize my chances of finding other employment.

A week hadn't yet gone by when I received a phone call from Houghton, offering to pay half of my expenses if I agreed to fly out for an interview. And, before a second week had passed, I was boarding a plane and heading for New York.

I felt good about the trip and kept close to the phone for the next two weeks, afraid that I might miss hearing from Houghton. I was ecstatic when the call came inviting me to work part-time in the Houghton College Career Development Center while completing a master's program at Buffalo. That's not a bad deal, especially considering how much I wanted to leave Thomson. I was asked to show up for work beginning the third week in August— three months later—and couldn't wait for the summer to end.

Some may say that I took the easy way out by leaving Thomson and moving to Houghton. I prefer to think of it as moving on to a more suitable profession. I'm not one to walk away from something just because it's a little harder than I expected it to be. I wouldn't have gotten anywhere in life if I had bailed out every time the going got tough. On the other hand, I don't believe in forcing something that isn't working. There's a time to stay in a job, stick it out, and hope things will improve. There's also a time to leave and to explore others options in life. The hard part is knowing when to stay and when to leave. For me, it was simply time to pack my bags and move on.

Fifteen

New York

If Houghton College didn't exist, the town of Houghton, New York would be about the same size as Thomson, Illinois. For the next two years, Houghton College would be the place I called home, and after being away for so long, it felt good to be back in the classroom. I had always enjoyed school, and this time I even applied myself, something I did not always do while at Taylor.

The student development program consisted of twelve classes, including two internships, stretched over four semesters. I had a 4.0 going into my second year, when I made one too many errors in writing up my major project proposal. That and the "B" I received during my fourth semester for failing to do an optional research paper brought my overall average down to 3.8. I simply didn't want to bother with the additional work required for an "A" in the class. The only difference would have been a tenth of a grade point in my overall GPA and a boost to my ego. I figured that my grades were high enough and that I could afford to live with a little less ego and spend a little more time socializing.

Six of us from Houghton College were enrolled in the graduate program at Buffalo State College, and we arranged our classes so that we only had to make the drive to Buffalo once a week. We would leave Houghton on Monday afternoon; attend a two-and-a-half hour class starting at 4:45; go to another one at 7:30; spend the night at Houghton's extension campus in West Seneca, New York; attend another class the next night; and then go home to Houghton. Our schedule made for a long, exhausting two days each week.

A real camaraderie existed among the grad students from Houghton. Maybe it was the shared experience during the winter months of braving the elements—the blizzards, whiteouts, and subzero temperatures—in order to make the hour-and-a-half trek to Buffalo each week. Perhaps it was the fact that all of us were enrolled in the same graduate program. Whatever the reason, most of us became pretty good friends during the two years that we were at Houghton.

Skip Trudeau was a year ahead of me in Houghton's student development program and was residence director of one of the dormitories on campus. Skip and I sometimes hung out together during our off hours, and every once in awhile, we ran into each other in the middle of the day.

"Have you started on that paper for Johnson's class?" I asked, one afternoon in the student union.

"I've thought about it, but that's about all I've done. How about you?"

"I started writing a couple of days ago."

"Goober," Skip said, with a touch of jealousy in his voice, "you always start early."

Why he called me Goober, I'll never know. But after pausing for a moment, he said it again.

"Skip," I protested. "Why are you calling me 'Goober'?"

"Goober," he said, feeling quite proud of himself. "I kind of like that."

There must be worse nicknames to have than "Goober," but none come to mind. I dreaded the thought of going through two years of graduate school with the same name that Gomer Pyle's cousin had in a television sitcom back in the 1960s. It was too late, though. Skip already had his mind made up. The name stuck, and within a couple of days, other people were using it too.

"Hey, Goober," another graduate student, Merna, asked one afternoon while passing me in the hall. "What are you doing tonight?"

"Just studying," I said. "The same thing I do every night."

"Do you have time to run me to the store?"

"Sure," I said, not knowing what I was letting myself get into.

We drove to the Market Basket in Fillmore, about four miles east of Houghton, for what I thought would be a quick trip to the grocery store.

"Don't they have what you need?" I asked.

"I can't decide which toothbrush to buy."

It took ten minutes for Merna to find the right toothbrush because, she said, she wanted the color to match her bathroom. I did not know that such finicky people existed. To me, a toothbrush is a toothbrush, and once I've decided on the kind of toothbrush I want, it doesn't matter whether it's red, green, or purple. It did matter to Merna, though. Everything had to be color-coordinated, right down to her toothbrush matching the hand towels in the bathroom.

There was something else unusual about Merna, besides the fact that she bought color-coordinated toothbrushes. She had the same last name as mine, a coincidence that led to plenty of confusion during the two years we were at Houghton together.

"I sure would like to meet your wife," Tom said, while pushing a broom down the hall of the campus center.

"I would too," I responded, letting Tom know that I wasn't married.

"You mean Merna's not your wife?"

"Nope."

"I thought that the two of you were married."

"Not to my knowledge," I said, jokingly.

Tom's mistake was a common one, and Merna and I grew accustomed to having to explain the nature of our marital status. The last thing that I needed as a single guy at Houghton was for everyone to think I was married. It had been a long time since I had lived on a college campus, and I meant to take advantage of having access to a campus full of young women.

Looking for a wife is a little like going fishing. You need the right kind of bait and a lot of patience. You can have a twenty-pound catfish on the line, but unless you know how to get fish into the boat, you might as well pack up your gear and go home. By the time I arrived at Houghton in the fall of 1986, I knew how to fish. Dating had become a science, and it was one at which I intended to excel.

I spent the first few months in New York just getting to know people, but when Steve Brooks asked me to house-sit during the first weekend in November, things really started cooking. Steve was Houghton's head basketball coach, and he needed someone to look after his dog, the lovable Dr. J., while he and his wife were out of town for a basketball tournament. I agreed and vowed to make good use of the house while they were away.

The first thing I did was ask Julie Miller for a date. Julie was a cheerleader for the basketball team and a resident assistant in one of the girls' dorms on campus. I invited her to watch a movie at Steve's house that Friday night and to take a trip over to Big Al's Pizza afterward. I really liked Julie and was kind of hoping that things might click between the two of us. We both liked the movie, *Murphy's Romance*, with James Garner and Sally Field. The pizza, with Canadian bacon and pineapple, was great. However, the date seemed to fizzle somewhere between the time I picked Julie up and the time we ordered our food. I took her home, said goodbye, and knew that would be my first, last, and only date with Julie Miller.

That was okay, though. The secret to good fishing is in not giving up. I still had a couple of good movies left, and the first thing I did on Saturday morning was look around for someone other than Julie to watch them with. I went over to Merna's apartment, told her about Julie, and asked if she knew of someone who might be interested in watching the movie *Amadeus* with me.

"I'm sorry things didn't go better for you last night."

"Thanks," I said, still a little disappointed that things hadn't worked out with Julie.

"I have a paper due on Monday," Merna added. "Otherwise, I would watch the movie with you myself."

"That's okay," I said, knowing that she had a lot of work to do.

"I've got an idea! What if I make an all-hall announcement?" she offered, just before walking out the door, down the hall, and into the office. "Attention East Hall girls!" I heard over the public address system. "Anyone interested in watching the movie *Amadeus*, please come down to the lounge."

I couldn't believe my ears. There must have been 300 beautiful young women in her dorm, and she was inviting all of them to watch a movie with me. It was my lucky day!

Three girls came to the lounge after Merna's announcement: Tami Tetrault, Sharon Combs, and Randi Mathisen. They all wanted to watch the movie, and the four of us agreed to meet at the lounge later that night to go over to Coach Brook's house.

When I drove back to the dorm a few hours later, I fully expected to spend the evening with all three girls, but to my surprise, both Tami and Sharon had found other things to do. That left Randi.

I didn't know much about Randi and had met her only once before. She was a senior psychology major, worked as a proctor at the East Hall desk, and had been wanting to see the movie *Amadeus* for some time. However, she hadn't planned on watching it with a guy she hardly knew—me—in the basement of a house where she had never been before.

For my part, I was interested only in watching a movie, having a good time, and doing a little bit of laundry. That's right. It was laundry night, and I stopped the movie every thirty minutes or so to go into the other room and throw another load into the washing machine. Not exactly the thing to do to impress someone on the first date!

Maybe I wasn't trying to impress Randi, but Randi sure impressed me. We hadn't said more than a couple of words to each other before that night, and yet after the movie we talked as though we had been best friends for years. She told me all about her classes, friends, and family, and I told her all about how I had ended up at Houghton. One of the first things I wanted to know was whether or not Randi was seeing anyone. I figured that if I asked her straight out, I might scare her off, so I told her about my breakup with Sandy. Sure enough, she followed my lead and told me about a couple of guys she had dated, but said that currently she wasn't seeing anyone. Just what I wanted to hear.

"How would you like to drive up to the school farm?" I suggested, not wanting the night to end.

Houghton is located in the foothills of the Allegheny mountains, and on a clear night, you can see for miles and miles across the valley. The sky was a bit overcast and the temperature was down around freezing—pretty typical for the beginning of November in western New York State. But despite the cold weather, Randi and I were like two kids on summer vacation. We walked around, looked at the horses, and kept right on talking.

Two days later, I showed up at Randi's dorm after dinner and asked if she wanted to go for another drive. She said yes, and we headed back to the farm. I half expected the spark I had felt earlier in the week to be gone. It wasn't, though, and we picked up exactly where we had left off—talking as if we had been best friends forever. Before the evening was over, I knew that Randi was someone I wanted to get to know better. I asked her to go to the play *You Can't Take It With You* the next Friday night, and once again she accepted my invitation.

"What did you think of the play?" I asked afterwards, getting ready to say good night.

"I liked it," Randi said, right before leaning over and kissing me on the lips. She then jumped out of the car and headed for the dorm, determined not to give me a chance to say anything. Amazed, I realized that Randi liked me. She was interested in more than a platonic friendship with just another guy. She wanted to date.

Randi had only one semester left before finishing at Houghton, and I knew that if our relationship was going to go anywhere, it had to happen soon. That's why I invited her to spend part of Christmas vacation with me in Wisconsin, something that stunned my parents and shocked Randi.

I had everything figured out. I would catch a ride home from New York with a friend of mine who lived in South Dakota. Randi would fly to Wisconsin after Christmas and spend time with me at my parents' house, and then John would pick us both up on his way back to Houghton. That's what we did—well, almost. I went home for Christmas, and Randi came a couple of days before New Year's. The night before we were scheduled to leave, John called.

"I sold my car, and I am flying back to New York," said the voice on the other end of the phone. "You and Randi will have to find another way of getting back to school."

John had left us stranded with no way of returning until the following Saturday, six days later, when my brother, Bill, drove us the 700 miles to Houghton. That was quite a trip, too. I had lain down in the back seat to get some sleep and wound up having motion sickness for most of the way to New York. I'll spare you the more gruesome details of the trip, but I will say that on more than one occasion Bill had to pull over so that I could take a walk alongside the ditch.

Despite the way the week ended, something magical happened between the time John called and the time Bill drove us to Houghton a few days later. Randi and I talked nonstop, sharing everything from our childhood memories to our dreams for the future. Before the week was over, I told her that I thought I was falling in love.

Some people have wondered how Randi could have let herself fall in love with someone with a disability. Of all the guys in the world, why pick one with cerebral palsy? No one plans to fall in love—it just happens. I'm not saying that my cerebral palsy was never an issue for Randi. She did give serious thought to whether she wanted to date someone with a disability. But once she made the conscious decision to date me, it didn't matter to her whether I was right-handed or left-handed, or tall or short, or disabled or not. She fell in love with the guy she was dating, and that was all there was to it.

I don't want to imply that Randi never had second thoughts about marrying me—because she did. Her questions never centered around the issue of my disability, though. Instead, they had more to do with her own insecurities about marriage itself. Randi's parents had divorced when she was seven, and the idea of marriage scared her. Subconsciously, she assumed that what had happened to her parents would eventually happen to her, too, and sometime after we became engaged, Randi started waking up in the middle of the night, wondering when I would leave her.

I don't share this to discredit Randi or members of her family. Rather, I share this to provide insight into the relationship between Randi and me. Randi did not wrestle with whether she could marry a man who has cerebral palsy. That was not the question. Instead, she wrestled with the idea of being married to a man—who happened to have cerebral palsy—who might leave her after a few years of marriage. There is a difference, and I hope that people see that difference. Fears of intimacy, change, and abandonment are exactly the same fears that all couples wrestle with when contemplating marriage—not just couples who have a disability. Marriage scared Randi, but her fears had nothing to do with my cerebral palsy.

Sixteen

In Sickness and in Health

Sometimes when I think about how I fell in love with Randi, I can't help but think about Sandy. At one time I had thought that I was in love with Sandy, yet this was different. I wasn't falling in love with Randi because I needed to. I was falling in love with Randi because I wanted to, and that made all the difference in the world. I had thought that I couldn't live without Sandy and discovered that I was miserable being with her. I knew I could live without Randi but realized that I didn't want to go through life without her. I had searched my whole life for someone to love and for someone to return that love, and Randi Mathisen was the person I had been searching for.

What makes a good marriage? To me, marriage is about being committed to your best friend. Without the commitment, and without the love and respect that go with that commitment, there is no marriage. Many people make the mistake of believing that love, romance, and great sex are the foundation of a good marriage. I'm all for love, I'm all for romance, and I'm very much in favor of great sex, but unless both people commit everything they have, are, and hope to be to each other, a marriage will not last.

I don't buy into the idea that a person is to serve God first, others second, and himself third. Although I am fully committed to loving God with all my heart, soul, and mind, God is not served in a vacuum. As far as marriage is concerned, the best way to serve God is to be totally, absolutely, 100% committed to one's mate.

When a person decides to marry, he (or she) is committing himself to making his spouse his number one priority in life, for life, with no exceptions. On May 21, 1988, Randi and I walked up the aisle of the Houghton Wesleyan Church as husband and wife. And the commitment I made that day to Randi is a commitment that I made for life. When I uttered the words "I will," I wasn't just committing myself to a lifetime of marriage. I was making a sacred vow to her that our relationship comes before my family, my work, my dreams, everything. That's what makes a good marriage—each partner vowing that kind of commitment to his or her best friend, period.

Now, after saying all that, I must tell you that on the morning after making that vow, I woke up with "cold feet." Randi had worked through all of her doubts before the wedding. I saved mine for the honeymoon. We had made our vows to each other a few hours earlier and had every intention of making those promises last a lifetime. However, we were both only in our twenties, and all of a sudden I wasn't quite sure that I wanted to spend the next fifty years being married to Randi. In fact, the very idea of being married scared me to death, and for the next two days I instinctively pulled inside of myself and put as much emotional distance between the two of us as possible.

You may think that my second thoughts might have put a damper on our first few days together. But Randi was determined not to let that happen. She was on her honeymoon and meant to enjoy every minute of it.

We had decided to spend a couple of days at Letchworth State Park, about twenty minutes up the road from Houghton. The Genesee River runs through the center of Letchworth, and huge canyon walls rise up on each side of its banks, forming a spectacular gorge. A wooden railroad trestle crosses the river at one end of the park, and an old-fashioned stone footbridge crosses it farther downstream near the bottom of the gorge. But the waterfalls are what really gives the park its character. There are three of them, and together they rival even the famous Niagara Falls, a hundred miles away, in beauty. We couldn't have asked for a nicer place to honeymoon. Everything was perfect. Everything, that is, except my fear of marriage, but that didn't last for more than a couple of days. It's a good thing, too, because after a very short honeymoon, Randi and I drove back to Houghton, where we spent the next few days packing.

Nothing can fully prepare a person for marriage. Not dating, not living together as some couples do, not anything. How can you take two people, each with his or her own quirks, character flaws, and separate likes and dislikes, bring them together, and then expect them to commit themselves to each other for the rest of their lives? We're talking major adjustment here. I was used to living by myself, but all of a sudden I'm living with this person who never leaves. And when she did leave, she always came back—to stay, with me, and in "my" apartment. She was there when I got up in the morning, and she was there when I went to bed at night. We ate together, slept together, and did almost everything else together. Randi is somewhat like cerebral palsy—she never goes away. Not that I ever really wanted her to. However, I used to at least be able to go into the bathroom alone. That place isn't even sacred anymore.

Marriage has been good for me. After having waited so long to find someone to fall in love with, having a wife who unconditionally loves me is—well, there's nothing like it. Yes, there was a period of adjustment. Yes, we did our share of arguing. But marriage brought healing to my life—to both of our lives. For Randi it brought a sense of stability that had been lacking since her parents' divorce. To me it brought a level of understanding and acceptance that I had never known before. Randi had made a conscious decision to spend the rest of her life with me, not because she had to, but because she wanted to. I found that to be tremendously healing as we started our new lives together as a couple.

When Randi and I crawl into bed at night and she wraps her arms around my body and holds me tight, something magical happens inside of me. Her touch brings healing to areas of my life so deeply scarred that I never dreamed wholeness in those areas was possible. Randi loves me. With every ounce of her being, she loves me. She loves me not despite my cerebral palsy, loving everything else and tolerating the disability, but with my cerebral palsy, loving my disability because it's so much a part of who I am.

Randi knows all too well the struggles I've experienced through the years because of my disability. She would love to see every trace of cerebral palsy gone from my life. However, her desires are not motivated by feelings of selfishness but by an all-encompassing love for me, Steve Chance, cerebral palsy and all.

I'm not saying that marriage has erased all of the bad things in my life. Deep down, I'm still the same guy I've always been. I still struggle with insecurities, and the shame that I felt while growing up has never totally left me. Having Randi in my life is a great help, however. Everyone should be as blessed as I am. She believes in me, and I can't imagine life without her.

Randi and I spent most of our engagement not knowing where we would be living once we were married. Then one weekend, we were suddenly faced with the need to make a quick decision. Randi had been on the waiting list earlier in the year for Rosemead School of Psychology, a graduate school of Biola University in La Mirada, California. She was called one Friday afternoon and told that she had until the following Monday to decide whether she wanted to enter the program. That was a tough weekend for us. Three days didn't give us much time to decide where we wanted to start our married life. At the time, I had been searching for work up and down the East Coast and in the Midwest. My field was student development, and I had just finished my master's program at Buffalo State. I had no job prospects in California, and if Randi accepted Rosemead's offer, we had no way of knowing whether or not I would find work. Finally, Randi and I decided that we would indeed move all the way across the country. We figured that if we let our fears get in the way of our dreams, we could spend the rest of our lives second-guessing our decision. So when Monday morning came, Randi placed the call to Rosemead, saying we would be in southern California in time for classes in the fall.

That was a whirlwind summer for us. We spent a week in Massachusetts, a week in Tennessee, and a couple of weeks in Wisconsin and Missouri before heading west. Our intentions were to spend time with family before moving so far away. We saw family, all right. I felt as though we had placed our marriage on hold during the summer and were just hanging on until we reached California and had a place to call home. Living with family is bad enough under normal conditions, but as newlyweds it was a nightmare. We were always either visiting friends or talking with family and never had time to ourselves. Things became so bad that one night we even left and found a hotel where we could finally be alone, without any distractions.

Driving across country should be another no-no when you're first married, especially driving a two-door Chevette with no air-conditioning. The Midwest was bad enough, but the desert was unbearable. Looking back on the trip, I don't know how we made it. Randi had had her driver's license for only a few months and wasn't used to long-distance car trips. That left me to do most of the driving. Now, I'll be the first to admit that my personality can take a sudden turn for the worse when I become overtired, and driving eight to ten hours a day for six days straight was almost more than I could handle. I remember stopping at the Grand Canyon and arguing afterward with my new wife about which of us would drive first. Randi wanted me to get us out of the crowded parking lot and said that she could take over from there. That sounds like a reasonable request, doesn't it? Not if you've been on the road for a week, are absolutely exhausted, and don't want to see anything but the inside of your eyelids for the next month.

Somehow we managed to finish the trip with our sanity intact, and by some miracle, we arrived in Norwalk, California sometime in the middle of the afternoon that next day. The race was on. We had $2000 left over from wedding gifts and $300 in monthly support raised to go toward the salary I would earn when beginning my new position at a local Youth for Christ chapter. Have you ever tried renting an apartment with no income except $300 in monthly pledges? Our friends said that it couldn't be done.

Our backs were against the wall, though, and we had to find a place to live before Randi started school.

We started walking along what is known as "apartment row" in La Mirada until we came across a vacant apartment that we both liked. The manager was noncommittal, but he told us to fill out an application and said that he'd get back to us. The very next day, he called to ask when we could move in. I couldn't believe it. After two-and-a-half months of marriage, we had our own apartment. It was small and cost more than three times what I had paid for an apartment in western New York, but it was ours.

One of Randi's big dreams in life was to become a licensed psychologist. I wholeheartedly supported that dream, so much so that the whole purpose of our moving to California was for her to attend Rosemead School of Psychology. However, if we had to make the decision again, Randi wouldn't attend Rosemead. It is a good school with a top-notch reputation in the Christian community, but that reputation has not been worth the price that we've had to pay for her to attend. And I don't mean just the financial cost of tuition, either. Although the debt we've accumulated over the years in student loans has been considerable, it pales in comparison to the toll that it's taken on our lives in other ways.

That first semester was pretty tough for us. Besides encountering all the adjustments that come with being newlyweds, there were all the additional pressures of school. I've been a student, and I've been to grad school, but I've never seen anything as demanding on a person's time, energy, and emotions as Rosemead. The doctoral program takes a minimum of five years, and the pressure to produce is horrendous. A student is allowed only two C's during those five years, and anyone who receives more is in jeopardy of being booted out of the program.

In addition to the academic demands, the financial burden placed on our marriage was astronomic. Tuition alone was more than $10,000 a year, and Randi had to take a part-time job, working twenty hours a week as the technical editor for the school's *Journal of Psychology and Theology*, just to make ends meet. Between work and studies, there was very little time for us as a couple.

As difficult as those early years were, our troubles really began shortly after the first of the year back in 1991, two-and-a-half years into Rosemead's program and soon after Randi had been awarded her master's degree. We had just returned from spending Christmas with family in the Midwest when Randi started having severe headaches and muscle aches. They were so bad that at times all she wanted to do was to take a couple of Advil and crawl back into bed until the pain went away. The problem, however, was that the headaches and muscle aches never did go away, and soon were compounded by debilitating fatigue. After a week or so went by, I took her to the Biola University Health Center. The doctor blamed her headaches on tension and gave her a muscle relaxant, which did absolutely nothing at all to relieve her pain.

The second doctor we went to, our family internist, made a diagnosis of mononucleosis. "I'll give her something for the headaches," she said reassuringly. "Randi can expect to feel better in about six months."

At the time, we were very much relieved with the "mono" diagnosis. A lot of people come down with mono. They're sick for a few months, but eventually they recover. I wish that things had been that simple. Little did we know then that Randi's headaches and fatigue were just the beginning of our problems.

A year went by with no visible signs of improvement, so we started looking elsewhere for answers. Randi's mother told us about a specialist in Anaheim Hills, about 45 minutes from where we lived, whose practice is limited exclusively to chronically ill patients. We made an appointment, and the doctor asked a lot of questions and ordered a battery of tests. After a few months, he finally gave a diagnosis: Randi has chronic fatigue and immune dysfunction syndrome, or CFIDS.[1]

Many people overexert themselves to the point of exhaustion. They go home, get a good night's rest, and by the next morning are ready to go again. People with CFIDS are different. It does not

---

[1] Pronounced "see-fids," this illness is more commonly known as chronic fatigue syndrome. As the newer name suggests, researchers have discovered that one of the effects of the illness is a malfunctioning immune system.

matter how much sleep or rest they have. They wake up feeling just as exhausted as when they went to bed the night before and then remain that way throughout the day.

There has been a lot of confusion over the nature of CFIDS— by the medical profession, the media, and the general public— since it was identified in the 1980s. Some confuse it with major depression, even though it has many characteristics that differentiate it from that illness. Others assume that the disease is psychosomatic, or "all in the head." The media has trivialized it by dubbing it the "yuppie flu," thereby dismissing the seriousness of the illness and implying that the people who suffer from it are lazy, upper-class hypochondriacs. Randi hates the term "yuppie flu," and I don't blame her. Randi is anything but lazy. She's bright and ambitious. And despite what the name of the illness might suggest, fatigue isn't the only symptom of CFIDS.[2] Randi also experiences severe headaches, insomnia, poor concentration, shortness of breath, difficulty in digesting food, sore throats, sinus problems, and muscle and joint pain and weakness—all attributed to the same illness. At times Randi is so weak from fatigue and so sore from muscle aches that she uses my old cane to walk.

There are days when all Randi can do is move into the living room, lie on the couch, and vegetate until it is time to go back to bed that night. Often she does not even have the energy to carry on a simple conversation, and we have sometimes gone through entire days without saying much more than a simple "How are you?" or "I love you!" to each other. On other days, she feels well enough to go out for a short time, only to come home afterward and collapse, spending the rest of the day either in bed or on the couch.

For the first few years, Randi and I assumed that her illness would be temporary. Eventually, we hoped, Randi would get well, and she would be able to graduate from Rosemead's program and resume her plans to become a psychologist. She was motivated,

---

[2] For more information about chronic fatigue and immune dysfunction syndrome, please contact: The CFIDS Association of America, P. O. Box 220398, Charlotte, North Carolina 28222-0398. Phone: 800-442-3437.

and very talented, and at the time, she had no intention of giving up her academic and professional dreams.

For over a year, Randi struggled to keep her job as the technical editor for Rosemead's *Journal of Psychology and Theology* while also maintaining her status as a full-time student. As soon as we were able to afford it, she quit her job and eventually cut her course load to part-time—taking only two classes per semester. Looking back, I don't see how she kept going. It's one thing to be tired. It's another thing entirely to live in a constant state of exhaustion while pushing yourself to work and attend school. Yet that's exactly what Randi did. She kept trying—hoping that by trimming enough off of her schedule, she could somehow continue.

When we moved to California in 1988, our plans had been for Randi to finish her doctoral program in five years and work full-time for at least a year or two after that; then we wanted to start a family. Because of CFIDS, none of that has happened. After years of missing classes and turning in late assignments, Randi and I finally realized that she would never be able to complete all of her graduation requirements—especially the more demanding ones, such as the internship and the doctoral thesis. Even more importantly, we also realized that she would never have any hope of physical recovery if she kept pushing her body beyond its limits.

Ever since high school, Randi had dreamed of becoming a licensed psychologist. Her last attempt to hold onto that dream was the year's leave of absence that she took from school, hoping that the added rest would quicken her recovery time. But when she was still ill at the end of that year, Randi finally came to terms with what had become inevitable; she quit her graduate program and gave up her career plans.

If someone had told me just how difficult coping with this illness would be, I probably wouldn't have believed them. I would have just blown them off, thinking that Randi and I were capable of handling anything. Although we are coping, the truth is that CFIDS has made life harder for us than we could ever have imagined.

One of the hardest things about Randi's illness is the isolation it causes. When she is at her worst, Randi sometimes goes for a week or more without seeing anyone except me. A couple of friends have stayed in contact with us and have made efforts to be helpful. Other friends, either because they do not understand the nature of Randi's illness or because they are simply too busy doing other things, have fallen by the wayside. One guy suggested that I simply tell Randi to snap out of it and get her act together. If only it were that easy. Another person told me that she doesn't believe she could stay married to someone who is chronically ill. Just the kind of encouragement that you want to hear when your mate has been ill for years.

Other friends have given us all sorts of advice, each proposing a different cure or solution to our problems. Although we appreciate their good intentions, we need friends who are willing to share the burden of Randi's illness with us, not advice on how to make her well. People from our church have helped with some of the practical tasks that we have trouble with, such as doing housework or running an occasional errand. One friend regularly takes Randi to get her hair cut; others check on her when I'm out of town. Three teenage girls invited themselves over one night last December; they brought us an artificial Christmas tree, put it up, and then decorated it. One time when Randi and I were both laid up with the flu, friends brought us groceries, cleaned up our kitchen, and even made us lunch.

As supportive as many people have been, however, we still struggle with loneliness. Randi's CFIDS makes if tough for us to get close to people. Most couples our age have parenthood in common, yet Randi and I have not been able to have children due to her illness. Working couples can usually socialize in the evening, whereas Randi is most alert in the afternoon. Randi's symptoms are very unpredictable, so we often have to cancel social plans—but rescheduling with busy couples often means that we may not be able to make plans again for a month.

In a lot of ways, it would be easier if we knew whether or not Randi will recover from this illness. Unfortunately, there is no consistent prognosis for CFIDS. We've met people who have recovered from CFIDS, and it's encouraging to see them working, raising families, and getting along just fine. Some people, though, remain ill indefinitely, with little or no improvement. As of this writing, Randi has been sick for over five-and-a-half years.

I wish there were some way that I could close this chapter on a more upbeat note. I can't. I simply don't know what the future has in store for us. I know that I love Randi, that she loves me, and that our commitment to each other is just as strong today as it was on the day we married. I know that God is a gracious God who has promised to go through life with us. He has not left us alone with this illness. Where we hurt, where we struggle, that's where God continues to meet us. Besides those two things, there isn't much else to know. There are no guarantees in life. That's part of what it means to walk by faith. Nevertheless, at times walking by faith isn't nearly as easy as it sounds.

Seventeen

One More Time

Two weeks after Randi and I committed ourselves to Rose-mead, I received a phone call from the executive director of a Youth for Christ chapter in southern California. "Steve, how would you like to come back to work for Youth for Christ?" Tony asked that day.

"Maybe," I said, trying to sound noncommittal. "How did you hear about our plans to move to California?"

"Scott Bellows told me about you. He gave me your resume and said you would be the perfect candidate to direct one of our new programs."

"What kind of program?"

"We want to begin a ministry for physically disabled teenagers and need someone to start it. Are you interested?"

"Sure, I'm interested," I said. "Let me think about it."

Randi and I were about to move 2500 miles away, and my phone call from Tony seemed to confirm our decision for Randi to attend Rosemead. I accepted his offer, began raising my financial support, and a couple of days after moving to southern California, showed up for my first day of work.

There's a part of me that says that I should have known better than to return to Youth for Christ. I had worked for YFC right out of college and, for a number of reasons, had vowed that I would never work with them again. My experience in Beloit had left such a bad taste in my mouth that I had wanted nothing to do with it or any other parachurch ministry. At the time, though, I really hoped that the YFC organization in California would be far different from the one in Wisconsin. And in some ways, it was different. It had a larger staff, a different director, a bigger budget, and more activities for kids to join. However, even with all of the good things going for it, the program was not what I had hoped that it would be.

The organization was massively in debt, a fact explained away by the fiscal irresponsibility of the previous director. By themselves, the past financial indiscretions didn't bother me, and I figured that the recent change in leadership would take care of any lingering budgetary problems. However, what I did not know was that the director and the board had little involvement with the staff. In fact, it wasn't until six months after my arrival that I met one-on-one with the director. Even then, our meeting had more to do with me personally and how I was getting along with everyone at the office than it did with ministry development. I don't want to imply that his interest in my personal life was necessarily a bad thing. It's just that I expected him to take a greater interest in my professional responsibilities, especially now that I had been on staff for six months.

The lack of organizational leadership was only one of my problems at YFC. I didn't know the first thing about establishing a ministry for disabled teenagers, and my year-and-a-half at this YFC proved it. That may sound strange coming from a man who has been disabled all of his life, but despite what some people might think, my cerebral palsy doesn't make me an expert in disability ministries.

I met with Herb Michael, a special education teacher in Santa Ana, and asked if he had any ideas about where I could start meeting kids.

"Why don't you come over to the school, and I'll introduce you to our principal?" Herb offered. "Mrs. Carter might know of something."

"You would be a great role model for some of our high school kids," Mrs. Carter said later that week. "There are 160 students between the ages of 3 and 21 in this school, and I know that many of them would like to meet you."

"When do I start?"

"How about tomorrow?" Herb suggested. "You can begin in my class around 1:00."

I drove down to Herb's school, Carl Harvey School for the Orthopedically Disabled, every Thursday afternoon for nearly two years. During that time, I tutored students in math, English, social studies, and science—anything, just to get my foot in the door and meet kids.

Tom was a junior and spent a part of each day at Carl Harvey and the rest of his day taking classes at Valley High School, across the parking lot. Tom had cerebral palsy and, like a lot of other kids his age, wanted to go to the prom.

"Why won't anyone go with me?" he asked one day, after telling me that he had invited several girls to the prom, only to be turned down repeatedly.

"Maybe you're asking the wrong girls?"

"Maybe," he said, with the sound of frustration in his voice. "I've already asked a lot of girls, though, and they've all said no."

"You're already doing a lot better than I did in high school," I said, after telling him about what had happened between Cindy Jackson and myself in the school cafeteria. "Don't give up. Sooner or later you're going to find someone to date. That's what happened to me." I didn't have the heart to tell him about Sandy Nolan's search for her dream man.

One week I went to the school only to find out that there had been a big argument a few days before between some of the older kids over at the high school and Dennis Bradley, one of the students at Carl Harvey.

"They were picking on me, Steve," Dennis complained, as soon as I walked into the room.

"Who?"

"Some kids over at the high school. They held my wheelchair so I couldn't go anywhere and then started teasing me."

That's when I told Dennis the story of Bobby Hogan, the kid who had picked on me during grade school. "There's going to come a day when you'll look back and laugh at the people who teased you this week," I told him. "You're going to make something out of your life. No amount of teasing will change that."

Dennis got the biggest kick out of hearing about Bobby. "Steve!" he would say every week for about a month. "Tell me the story of when you and Bobby were in grade school."

"I just told you that story a few days ago. Why do you want to hear it again?"

Dennis would look up at me from his chair and, with a big grin across his face, say, "Because I like it."

I'm one who believes that a great deal of ministry comes out of just spending time with people. In fact, some of the greatest opportunities I've ever had in ministry have come from simply making myself available to people. That's why I decided to begin a weekend club program for a couple of the teenagers from Carl Harvey, a few months after I first started visiting there. Every Saturday morning, I drove down to Orange County, picked up the kids, and brought them to the house of one of the students to talk about everything from school, to dating, to having a personal relationship with Jesus Christ.

I remember one girl in particular. Becky Sanders·had cerebral palsy and, for some reason, never said much when I was around. She always answered my questions with two- or three-word sentences and never volunteered anything without being asked. However, Amy Bleam, one of my student volunteers from Biola University, had the ability to bring Becky out of her shell, and when the two of them were together, Becky became a different person.

A group of us went to the park one afternoon. "That looks like fun," Amy said, eyeing the monkey bars a few feet away. That was all the encouragement Becky needed, and before another word was said, we were making our way to the other side of the park. It took three people to help Becky climb up those bars—two to support her balance and one to position her feet. Becky made it to the top, and the look on her face told us that she was having the time of her life.

I discovered the significance of that afternoon a few days later. "Did you know that Saturday was the first time Becky had ever played on monkey bars?" Amy asked, on our way over to Carl Harvey.

"It's amazing how much we take for granted," I said, knowing how some kids with disabilities are sheltered. "Who would have guessed that a simple thing like going to the park would have made such a impact on Becky. She'll remember that day for the rest of her life."

Despite the way that God blessed my time with the small group of kids that showed up on Saturday mornings, I grew discouraged during the course of that first year at this YFC, both by the lack of support that I received from our executive director and by my own lack of experience. That's when I began seeking the advice of people who knew more than I did about disability ministries.

Of all the people I talked with, Bob Pietsch was the most helpful. Bob had been a Presbyterian minister for most of his life before founding an organization called ADD (Advocates with people who are Developmentally Disabled). Bob's own son had been developmentally disabled, and ADD was born out of Bob's desire to see churches include Larry and other people with developmental disabilities into their ministry.

Bob inspired me. He had successfully taken the events of his own life—the birth, disability, and death of his son Larry—and turned them into opportunities for ministry. After seeing the impact that Bob had on area churches in helping them develop ministries with disabled people, I knew I wanted to do the same thing. I could use my cerebral palsy as a starting point for ministry and, by doing so, could impact a lot of people with the love and grace of Jesus Christ.

Bob affirmed my dream of one day starting a ministry independent of any other organization. He reminded me that if God was really behind what I was doing, then I would somehow find a way to make it happen. "Feel free to talk to me any time you want," Bob said. That was good news, especially since I was about to embark on one of the biggest undertakings of my life.

After what amounted to a little over a year of working at the southern California YFC, I decided to leave. I went to the library and read everything that I could find about how to start a non-profit organization. I typed out the bylaws and articles of incorporation, mailed in the application, and waited three months before receiving approval from the California Secretary of State to begin operation.

Golden Clay Ministries was born out of a conviction that every person, regardless of racial background, ethnicity, gender, socio-economic level, or physical and mental limitations, has been created in the image of God. Unfortunately, that image has been tarnished by sin and can only be restored by Jesus Christ. He alone brings value to our lives. My worth doesn't come from being able to walk straight, because I can't. My worth doesn't come from being able to hold a glass of water without spilling it, because I can't do that either. My worth comes from one thing and one thing alone—knowing Jesus Christ. He is the one who takes the ugliness of my life and transforms me from a broken, clay vessel into a creature of infinite worth.

Eighteen

Speaking Out

My first big break came a few months after I left YFC, when a church of two thousand members invited me to preach during their annual Disability Awareness Sunday. Their pastor of twenty years, a very intellectual and educated man, had just resigned. His approach to ministry was very cerebral, and each of his sermons reflected his high level of intelligence. Yet, even with all of his academic training, he had been unable to speak to the emotional needs of the people in his congregation. As a result, although church members had been routinely treated to scholarly messages on Sunday mornings, they had been discouraged from expressing any feelings of pain or sorrow that they may have been dealing with during the week.

That's where I came in. I was asked specifically to help the congregation experience some of the emotions that had been unexpressed for years. I was given forty-five minutes to speak during the morning service—time enough, I was told, for only a short sermon.

My cerebral palsy was very evident as I worked my way to the pulpit that morning, and I could almost hear the apprehension in the minds of the people watching me. The auditorium held nearly 1200 people, and in both services, you could have heard a pin drop as I spoke openly of my struggles with a God who sometimes allowed my prayers to go unanswered, as well as of the triumphs and breakthroughs of a journey that began with an acute shortage of oxygen to the brain at birth.

I candidly talked about how I had seen myself as being un-datable in high school and then about Sandy and all the trouble I had had while the two of us were dating. I told everything from how she had taped the picture of her ideal man—not me—to the refrigerator door, to the Sunday afternoon when she had asked me to walk straighter. Although having a congregation of that size wanting to lynch my former girlfriend might have been good for my ego, my intentions were not to lash out at Sandy. Instead, I wanted to help everyone in that auditorium to recognize his or her own agony in life.

"Whether it's divorce, the death of a spouse, unemployment, or life with a rebellious teenager who's out of control," I said, "everyone has experienced pain in one form or another."

I turned from talking about myself to talking about Christ.

"Sometimes we minimize Jesus' humanity, and we shouldn't. Christ was publicly stripped and beaten, nailed to a cross, and then left for dead. His pain was just as real to him as yours is to you and mine is to me," I said. "God doesn't condemn our moment of despair and unbelief. Christ himself pleaded to escape the cross and, on it, cried out in agony."

I then went to the heart of my message. "I believe," I contin-ued, "that in our attempt to bring healing to the broken areas of our lives, we ask the wrong question. Instead of asking, 'How can we make our pain disappear?' we should more appropriately ask, 'How can we experience the grace of God in the midst of our great-est pain?'"

I finished with a prayer and made my way off the platform. I was completely overwhelmed by what happened next. I was sit-ting beside a pastor who had earlier expressed doubts about my coming, and he was so moved by what I had said that he was in tears, not just allowing a little tear to trickle down his cheek, but openly and unashamedly crying his heart out. He wasn't alone. Dozens of people approached me afterward to thank me for a message that had deeply moved them. Some were so filled with emotion that it was all they could do to look at me, shake my hand, and walk away, making room for the next person standing in line.

My goal that morning was to infiltrate some of the deepest and most painful areas of people's lives with the healing grace of Jesus Christ. I had put forty hours into preparing my message, and if the things that people were telling me after the service were any indication of what was going on in the hearts of the rest of the congregation, then I knew that my efforts had paid off.

That morning was a good one for me, and I fully expected that afterwards I wouldn't have to work so hard at lining up additional speaking engagements. That expectation turned out to be somewhat exaggerated. Although it's true that a certain number of invitations to preach in other churches did come my way as a result of the success of that morning, I still faced the task of having to prove myself to most of the church leaders I contacted.

I understand the need for pastors to scrutinize prospective speakers. If I still had my own church, I would be very careful about who I invited to fill the pulpit. That's the job of a senior pastor—to make sure that the congregation receives the best teaching possible. I fully endorse that type of inquiry and invite pastors to examine my credentials, including my ability to communicate effectively with my audience. I also do not want to assume that every church I approach should automatically invite me to preach. God has his own timing for things, and perhaps his plans do not include my speaking at a particular church.

However, having said that, let me also say that I have been discriminated against by both pastors and other church leaders who, solely because of my disability, refused to even consider allowing me to speak in their church service or Sunday school class.

Before I approach any pastor or Sunday school teacher about preaching or teaching in a church, I always obtain either a written recommendation or a verbal endorsement from a mutual friend such as Joni Erickson Tada, of JAF Ministries; Jay Kesler, president of Taylor University and past president of YFC; or Eric Heard, youth pastor at Fullerton Evangelical Free Church.

None of these people are exactly lightweights within the Christian community. Both Jay Kesler and Joni Erickson Tada are nationally recognized, and Eric Heard has worked for years as the senior high youth pastor at Chuck Swindoll's former church in southern California.

It seems reasonable to expect that with endorsements such as those, most people would at least take the time to talk with me. Most do. However, every once in a while, I run into someone who, for one reason or another, appears to have a real problem with my disability.

I made an appointment one afternoon to see the director of Christian education at a medium-sized church in Orange County, California. I arrived at her office, carrying the appropriate endorsements, but to my dismay, I was written off before I even had a chance to sit down. She had agreed to see me, all right, but our meeting was short and straight to the point.

"We have our own staff of volunteers to teach the Sunday morning classes," she said, making it very clear that the church wouldn't be needing my services.

Not being one to give up easily, I inquired if her teachers ever took vacations.

"Yes," she acknowledged. "They usually take four weeks off during the summer, but the church always finds replacement teachers."

I thought about asking if she would consider using me as a substitute teacher but decided against it. She had already made up her mind, and any further questions on my part would only prolong our conversation needlessly.

I had similar difficulties a year or so later when talking with a Sunday school teacher of another nearby church. I called on the advice of a well-known member of the congregation who assured me that I would make an ideal teacher for this particular class. All I needed to do, he said, was contact the class president and set up a time to teach. So that's what I did, but it wasn't quite as easy as my friend had made it sound. I called the class president, explained the reason for my call, and then asked if there might be a time when I could share my Sunday school series with her class.

"Maybe," she said. "Let me talk with a couple of people, and I'll call you back in a few days."

After a couple of weeks went by without hearing from her, I called again. That's when things started getting interesting.

I asked her whether or not she had had the opportunity to discuss my teaching her Sunday school class with anyone. She said that she hadn't. I told her that I understood and then asked when it would be convenient for me to call her back. She didn't know, and when I asked for the name of the person who had the authority to invite me to teach, she said that no such person existed. That sounded a bit odd to me, so that's when I decided to probe a little deeper. When I asked for the name of the person in charge of scheduling teachers, she was furious.

"I'm the class president," she said, clearly irritated. "I'm the one with the responsibility for lining up teachers."

"Okay," I said. "Would you consider having me teach your class?"

"I can't do that, at least not without talking to other class members first."

I was upset, she was upset, and around and around we went. I assured her that I did not want to upset her, and again asked her to give me the name of the person who would have the authority to invite me. Once more, she couldn't do that, because no such person existed.

The problem for me wasn't that this woman didn't want me teaching her Sunday school class, or that she needed time to check out my credentials, or even that her class wasn't interested in what I had to offer. She could have told me any of those things, and that would have been fine with me. The problem was that this woman wasn't being honest with me. For whatever reason, she chose to give some far-fetched excuse rather than tell me about the real problem.

After talking for another five minutes or so, we reached a compromise. I could come and give my testimony to the Sunday school class, but anything more was out of the question. That didn't make much sense, either. If she had the authority to invite me to use a full Sunday school hour to give my testimony, surely she had the authority to invite me to teach. I knew when to leave well enough alone, and even though I hate the idea of showing up someplace and giving the "disabled super-Christian" talk, I

thanked her for the invitation and agreed to come, in the hope
that further ministry opportunities might come my way as a result.

I think my performance that morning caught her a little off
guard. The entire class sat riveted to their seats as I told the
story of what life is like for a man with cerebral palsy. After I finished my testimony, the first person to approach me was this
woman's husband. He was so impressed by what I had said that
he wanted me to return on the following Sunday and share more
with the class. I was flattered and have to admit that, after all
the tension that had existed between me and his wife during the
previous couple of months, I found his invitation to be very gratify-
ing. Unfortunately, I already had a prior commitment to be at
another church on the following Sunday and couldn't return.

What about this man's wife? She came to me, after everyone
else had left the room, and rather sheepishly praised me for a job
well done. I thanked her for the kind words and left the classroom knowing that my words had changed the way that this
woman perceived people with disabilities.

I'm well aware that many people prejudge me and assume
that my cerebral palsy precludes effective communication from behind the pulpit. I suppose it's only natural to think that a person
who has difficulty doing a lot of other things in life would also
have difficulty speaking in public. What would happen if I walked
up to the podium, lost my balance, and fell off the platform?
What if, in the middle of my sermon, I begin drooling all over my
notes, embarrassing myself and everyone else in the auditorium?
Or, for that matter, what if I just did not have what it takes to
hold people's attention while speaking and bored the socks off of
everyone listening?

I know that I may come across as a little self-serving by making this next statement, and I don't mean to. Because I'm aware
of the prejudice that does exist in the minds of some people regarding my capabilities to address an audience, I want it known,
even if I'm the one saying so, that I'm very good at what I do. At
the risk of sounding conceited, let me assure you, in the strongest
possible terms, that I never stand up in front of a group of people
without commanding the full attention of everyone in the room.

God has gifted me, and when I get behind a podium and open my mouth to speak, people listen. That's just the way it is. I'm good at what I do, and I'm especially good when I'm in front of an audience.

Oh, sure, just like anyone else who regularly speaks to groups of people, I, too, have days when I'm not at my very best. Even on my off days, though, I'm still very good. And when I'm at my best, nothing can stop me from clearly articulating my thoughts in a way that moves the listener to the core of his or her being. I don't make these statements lightly, nor do I want to imply that I'm God's gift to the pulpit. I'm not. However, I've worked hard over the years to develop my ministry skills, and I am proud of my ability to speak directly to the hearts of people.

Nineteen

Pat Answers

Writing this book has been one of the hardest things that I've ever done. I started by asking a heart-wrenching question: Where was God during the first few minutes of my life as I lay suffocating on the delivery table? Even though I have made a lot of progress, I still lack many of the answers to some of my most basic questions about God and the way he works in the lives of those he loves.

Having cerebral palsy doesn't make me an expert on the sovereignty of God. I haven't resolved the issue of pain and suffering in the world, nor have I come up with the definitive answer to the question of why some people are born with disabilities and others are not. I have asked these questions for years, and most of the answers given to me by well-meaning Christian friends are all but worthless. They remind me of a man I met a few years back during a camping trip that I went on in the High Sierra mountains of California.

Twenty-five of us had gathered to experience five days of rock climbing and rappelling, an ambitious trip, especially considering the fact that six of us were disabled and four of those, including Paul, used wheelchairs. There is nothing like camping out on the side of a mountain, sleeping under the stars, and freezing at night to make a person appreciate some of the comforts of home. Our food was dehydrated, the water had to be purified, and the outhouse consisted of a bucket beneath a lawn chair with a toilet seat duct-taped to it.

The first thing that I noticed about Paul, besides the fact that he used a wheelchair, was his weight. I would never poke fun of someone just because of body size, and that certainly isn't my intent here. However, it's not every day that you hear about someone who weighs close to 250 pounds, and who uses a wheelchair, going rock climbing and rappelling. I assure you that it was no easy task taking Paul on this trip. Six staff members labored for two hours carrying Paul up the side of the mountain, and that was just to get him from the road to where we made camp. You can just imagine what it was like helping him rappel down the side of a 90-foot cliff.

There are two more things about Paul that you need to know in order to appreciate this story. First, Paul was the camp jokester and loved to make people laugh. I pride myself on my ability to tell a good joke, but even I took a back seat to Paul's quick wit. No one was safe from his dry humor, and he took advantage of every chance that he had to make us laugh. The second thing that you need to know about Paul is that he does not believe in God, and he makes no bones about it. It's not that he's antagonistic toward those who disagree with him. Just the opposite. He got along great with everyone on the trip and even welcomed opportunities to talk about questions of faith.

Most of our group were professing Christians, and Paul knew exactly where each of us stood in terms of our belief in God. In fact, he seemed to enjoy bantering good-naturedly with the rest of us. He even smiled when I invited him to follow me to the edge of the cliff so that I could ask him if he was ready to become a Christian. He declined my request, saying that he would not be believing in God at the top of the cliff and doubted very much whether he would at the bottom, either, if and when I pushed him over the edge. Just my luck—an atheist who isn't afraid of heights.

Along about the fourth day of the trip, I asked Paul about his belief or, in his case, his lack of belief in God. His answer surprised me. I half expected Paul to blow off my question with one of his usual one-liners. Instead of taking the opportunity to give me another one of his wisecracks, he answered me seriously. He told me that he could give a lot of reasons for not believing in God, but everything hinged on one problem: He could not understand why good people suffer. How could a loving and all-powerful God sit back and let someone like himself deteriorate from a disability? Paul had done nothing to cause his disability. Yet he will spend the rest of his life using a wheelchair.

What do you say to a guy who refuses to believe in a God who allows people to be disabled for life? I certainly didn't have the answer. My mind raced through everything that I had ever learned about the scriptures, apologetics, and the sovereignty of God. I knew all of the theological arguments about sin and free will. Yet none of those things seemed appropriate, and after a few moments of silence, I finally told Paul that sometimes life just stinks. Pretty brilliant, huh? The guy who's supposed to have all the answers, and my best comeback was to say that life stinks.

I'm sure many Christians would say that I blew it with Paul. After all, he left the door wide open for me to share what God has done in my life, and to assure him that God could do the same in his life, if given the chance. That was not what Paul was looking for, though. He wasn't asking for a thirty-second explanation about the problem of good and evil. Nor was he looking for pie-in-the-sky platitudes about a God who miraculously shields us from pain. Such a God doesn't exist in my own life, and even if he did, I doubt whether Paul would have been interested in such a plastic dime-store deity.

It's too easy to give pat answers—as though there is a magical hat filled with all the answers to all the questions that Christians will ever be asked. Whenever people get in a tight spot, all they have to do is reach into the hat and pull out the latest in Christian jargon. I'm sure that you've already heard all of the so-called answers before. I know I have—plenty of times. I've even used some of them myself: "If only you would trust God, things would get better." "If only you had a little more faith, things would change." Or, how about my all-time favorite, "If only you would just pray about it, everything would work out"? Don't get me wrong. I'm all for prayer, I'm all for faith, and I'm all for trusting

God. The question is: What happens after you pray and pray and pray, and you believe and believe and believe, and the problems that haunt you refuse to go away?

I've wrestled with these questions for most of my life, and for me everything comes down to the question of how I see God. Our modern-day culture has prostituted our image of God. When some people are asked to describe God, the first image that comes to their minds is the character played by Charlton Heston in *The Ten Commandments*. To these people, God is a little like Moses, only bigger, more glamorous, and more powerful. He is the great protector, the big grandfather in the sky—complete with a white beard and long, flowing robe—who stands ready to parcel out one favor after another to anyone he chooses.

Others see God as a deified vending machine who stands ready to dispense anything and everything asked of him at a moment's notice. The only thing that's required is to pray in a specific order—and then presto! Out comes the desire of one's heart. Perhaps there's even a cosmic drive-through window called McGod's, where one can order a hamburger, fries, and a miracle with the works. Wouldn't that be something to write home about? I could get rid of my cerebral palsy and order a Big Mac, all with the same prayer.

You're right! I am poking fun at the stereotypical images that society uses to portray the God of the universe, and I am exaggerating, just a little, the way that many people respond to those images. That's precisely my point. We've allowed both Hollywood and our own imaginations to warp our perception of who God really is. Either we think of God as a type of Superman who fights for truth and justice and answers our prayers on a moment's notice, or else we think of him as someone wearing oversized combat boots and standing ready to stomp on the first person who steps out of line.

I stumbled across an Iranian proverb a few years ago: "If you see a blind man, kick him. Why should you be kinder than God?" Now, before you recoil in shock, let me remind you that although we aren't quite as blatant with our theology, some well-meaning Christians assume that if a person is suffering, God must want it that way. I wish I had a nickel for every time someone has told me that it is God's will for people to suffer. I've even had Christians go so far as to tell me how fortunate I am that God made me disabled. They see the work that I'm involved in and assume that God gave me cerebral palsy to better equip me for ministering with other disabled people. I wonder whether they also think that God gave disabilities to those other people just so that I would have someone to minister to!

I do not believe that God causes suffering. There was no sickness or disability in the Garden of Eden. That came later, when Adam and Eve turned their backs on God and decided to go their own way. That wasn't God's decision. The reality is that we live in a fallen world, and suffering is one of the results of living in that fallen world. To try to pin the blame on God for the sufferings of the world is ultimately to blame God for sin.

Does God use my disability? Absolutely! I am extremely thankful for the way that God has chosen to use my life. However, there is a difference between God's *using* my disability to minister to other disabled people and his *causing* my disability specifically for that purpose. God does not have a quota system in which he parcels out disabilities at will!

If God does not cause disabilities to occur, then I am still left with the question, "Where was God when I was struggling to take my first breath at birth?" Many people would say that God was nowhere to be found, but I don't believe that. I believe he was there all along—with me through every struggling gasp of air I tried to take. Knowing that he had planned life, my life, to be good, healthy, and abundant, and knowing that humanity destroyed that life with sin, I believe that God was in the delivery room crying his eyes out, mourning the cerebral palsy that I would have to contend with all of my life.

I believe that a day is coming when God will dry every tear from the eyes of the faithful. As a man with cerebral palsy, that belief gives me tremendous hope. I've heard friends talk about how much they're looking forward to walking on streets of gold and living in a huge mansion. They paint heaven as a glorified Disneyland, complete with swimming pools, Jacuzzis, and eighteen-hole golf courses. I'm sure that heaven will be far more beautiful than we can ever imagine, but none of that glitter really appeals to me. What does appeal to me is knowing that one day I will no longer be disabled. I won't have cerebral palsy in heaven, and those of my friends who are disabled here on earth won't have to use wheelchairs or other devices to assist themselves. There will be no stopping us. We won't be stuck outside, waiting for some angel to install ramps to make heaven accessible. We will be walking and running and jumping and shouting "Hallelujah!" at the top of our voices, and everyone, and I do mean everyone, will know that Jesus Christ is Lord! I yearn for the day when I will stand face to face with Christ in a fully restored body and hear him say, "Well done, good and faithful servant" (Matt. 25:23, RSV).

That day isn't here yet, and no matter how much I wish things were different, the fact is that today, right now, at this point in time, I still have cerebral palsy. The good news is that I am not alone. God has not abandoned me. My hope comes from knowing that God will never leave me, no matter how desperate my life becomes. That's the one thing I can count on, no matter what. God loves me and is with me. Somehow that's enough. That has to be enough, because ultimately that is all there is, and to wish for anything more is to wish in vain.

I don't want to imply that we have no need of other people in our lives, or that we should feel like martyrs because of the hardships we face in life. I do need to share my life with people who are close to me. I have a wife, and I love her very much. I have friends I can turn to when life gets tough. However, friends move, loved ones die, and disasters happen. Ultimately, the one thing, the only thing, that will never change is God's commitment to me. God will never leave me, and that is my one and only hope.

Each of us has been at the end of his or her rope with nothing left to hang onto except memories of better times and a God who seems to be nowhere. The depression is overwhelming, the loneliness is unbearable, and some of the advice from those who try to help is all but worthless. I'm tired of hearing easy answers. People have a Band-Aid mentality toward God. They believe that by saying the right prayers and having enough faith, they will have a life filled with complete joy, with no pain or suffering of any kind. That is simply not true.

I believe that God does not offer easy answers to the tough questions that we ask about all the pain and suffering in the world. Instead, he offers us a relationship with Jesus Christ. There is a difference between the two. We've mistaken our relationship with Christ as a cure-all for pain and expect our lives to be filled with complete joy once we accept him as our savior. Yet, Jesus Christ did not die on the cross to take away my pain in life, at least not on this side of heaven. Christ died to take away my sins, and hallelujah, he's done that! He willingly faced the cross, died an agonizing and humiliating death, and arose from the grave three days later. Christ died for my sins, and I will be eternally grateful for his act of compassion on my behalf. But to assume that the purpose of Christ's death, burial, and resurrection was to provide a life of comfort somehow devoid of any and all types of pain and suffering is simply wrong.

Some may ask, "What good is a relationship with Jesus Christ if I'm still left to suffer?" I believe that it does a lot of good. Christ knows firsthand what it means to suffer. Pain is not an abstract theory that he learned from reading a textbook while basking in glory on the far side of heaven. He experienced it while hanging on a cross. It is because of that experience that he understands the hopelessness that comes when suffering seems inevitable.

When all is said and done, that's the Christ I want—not someone removed from all the hurts of the world, but someone who can identify with me and who knows what it's like to go through intense agony. It's precisely because of that firsthand knowledge of what it means to suffer that Christ refuses to offer me easy answers. He offers me a relationship with himself instead. And it's in that relationship that Christ offers me hope as I walk humbly with my God.

Epilogue

I first became aware of the need for disabilities ministry when I was living in New York. Sharlini De Mel, a Houghton College student, wanted to take a team of people on a mission trip to her home town in Sri Lanka. I agreed to help her plan the trip, and together we raised close to $14,000, enough to send her and six other students to Sri Lanka for two months that following summer.

"You're planning on going with us, aren't you Steve?" Sharlini asked one afternoon, after most of the money had been raised.

"I really want to go," I said. "But I'm not sure yet if I'll be able to make the trip."

"You have to go," Sharlini protested. "The people over there need someone like you."

"Why do you say that?"

"Steve," she said, "if you're disabled and live in Sri Lanka, you have nothing. Life is horrible. There are no jobs. The government doesn't help. You spend twelve hours a day sitting on the street corner, begging for money. If you are lucky, you have enough collected at the end of the day to buy some food that night. If not, you go to bed hungry and hope that the next day will be better."

I never made it to Sri Lanka, but I had the opportunity a few years later to see something similar to the deplorable conditions that Sharlini had spoken about. Nine of us had traveled to Mexico City for one of Golden Clay Ministries' short-term mission trips, and the day we visited one of the homes that house many of Mexico's severely disabled left an indelible mark on my memory. The first thing to catch my eye was the building itself, which looked more like an institution than a home. As many as a dozen kids slept in each of its many dormitory-style bedrooms. The bunks lining the walls reminded me of a medium-security prison that I had once visited in Attica, New York, where the inmates were warehoused and purposely kept away from the rest of society. The fence surrounding the yard of the home, although necessary to provide security for the kids, added to the prison motif.

Many of the residents had been abandoned in infancy and left to the care of the state by parents either unwilling or unable to raise a disabled child. The state, in turn, had handed them over to the Sisters of Charity who, as a last resort, had brought them to this facility. Our visit reminded me of what a man from Madagascar had once told me. "In my country," he had said, "the same word used for disability is also used to refer to the garbage that people throw out at the end of the day." Unfortunately, that is a very accurate depiction of how the kids in this home.are perceived by the outside world.

The needs of people with disabilities in such places as Sri Lanka and Mexico City are heart-wrenching and dramatic. But the needs of disabled Americans are great, as well. We need to be less marginalized, less isolated, and much more evangelized. People with disabilities are the largest minority group in the United States. There are more of us in this country than there are African-Americans, Latinos, or any other group. Yet, there are also fewer of us who attend church regularly compared with the members of any other minority group. That disturbs me, and if you truly believe that the love and grace of our Lord is meant for all people, it should disturb you, too.

I believe that God has called me to use my own life to communicate his grace to both disabled and non-disabled people. I am grateful for the work that Golden Clay Ministries is doing to help

churches integrate people with disabilities into their congrega-
tions. But no matter how many books I write, or sermons I
preach, or classes I teach—I can't make a difference in the lives of
more than a handful of people with disabilities without your help.
My message won't mean much unless ordinary Christians who
hear it put the muscle of their own effort behind my words. So, at
the risk of sounding like I'm preaching a sermon, I close this book
with a challenge. Open your church to people with all kinds of
disabilities. Make sure the sanctuary is accessible, but don't stop
there. If you work with someone who has a disability, invite that
person to attend church with you. Provide transportation for people who don't drive. Visit the ill who have trouble leaving their
homes—both elderly people and younger people like my wife,
Randi. Baby-sit a disabled child so that his or her parents can
get a night out to themselves. But most of all, give the gift of your
friendship. Let people with disabilities know that you want them
as a part of your congregation. Let your church be to many people
with disabilities what Youth for Christ was to an insecure teenager named Steve Chance in the 1970s—a place to belong.

Golden Clay Ministries

I dream of the day when I can look back on my life and see literally thousands and thousands of churches across America and around the world intentionally ministering to people with disabilities. If you have been moved by this book, if the heart strings of your life have been touched by the words you have just read, I urge you to join with me by becoming a financial partner of this important ministry. Golden Clay Ministries is a non-profit charitable organization that exists thanks to the generosity of our friends and supporters.

Thank you for your partnership!

☐ Mr. ☐ Mrs. ☐ Ms. ☐ Rev./Mrs. ☐ Mr./Mrs.

First Name(s) _____

Last Name _____

Address _____

City _____ State ____ Zip _____

Phone (_____) _____

☐ Yes! I want to support the work of Golden Clay Ministries. Enclosed is my tax-deductible gift in the amount of: _____

Wisconsin Address: P. O. Box 245 • Orfordville, WI 53576